Reclaim Your Life

The journey from wounded inner child to free-spirited woman

Karen Howe

Reclaim Your Life: The journey from wounded inner child to free-spirited woman © Karen Howe 2020

www.karenhowe.com.au

The moral rights of Karen Howe to be identified as the author of this work have been asserted in accordance with the Copyright Act 1968.

First published in 2020 by Karen Howe.

ISBN 978-0-6488067-6-9

Any opinions expressed in this work are exclusively those of the author and are not necessarily the views held or endorsed by Karen Howe.

All rights reserved. No part of this publication may be reproduced or transmitted by any means, electronic, photocopying or otherwise, without prior written permission of the author.

Disclaimer

All the information, techniques, skills and concepts contained within this publication are of the nature of general comment only and are not in any way recommended as individual advice. The intent is to offer a variety of information to provide a wider range of choices now and in the future, recognising that we all have widely diverse circumstances and viewpoints. Should any reader choose to make use of the information herein, this is their decision, and the author and publisher/s do not assume any responsibilities whatsoever under any conditions or circumstances. The author does not take responsibility for the business, financial, personal or other success, results or fulfilment upon the readers' decision to use this information. It is recommended that the reader obtain their own independent advice.

Dedicated to my Mother Ann Barber who has loved me unconditionally and who took care of me through thick and thin. To my soulmate Jeff Howe and my sons Matthew Shoesmith and Dylan Howe for reminding me the importance of sharing my gift to the world.

Foreword

I have known Karen Ann for 20 years. When we met, we were work colleagues and at the time Karen was recently single. We have worked together most of our 20 years and I am confident that we have a good friendship and a good working relationship. One doesn't affect the other. I can trust that Karen will always do what she says she will do.

At the very beginning when I met Karen, she was a single mother. I was pleasantly surprised that Karen wasn't helpless. My experience with single mothers in the past has been one of the helpless people trying to get their life together. Karen took her son overseas in the early stages and I was surprised that she could do this, so independently, so early in her new single life. She clearly thought, this is what we need, so let's just do it!!

When she told me she was writing a book to help others that have had similar experiences and bring something that resonates to the people to create true meaning and purpose in their lives, this was no surprise to me as Karen is a sharer. She is open and honest in her book, so warts and all, you will get to meet the real her.

She has had a lot of challenges in her life, but most of the time people aren't aware of them. That tells me she is fiercely independent, which is the women I met 20 years ago, and will be the woman I will get old with.

Karen is always cheerful and if you need someone to cheer you up, she is the right person to go to. Her business mind is always on. She can enjoy a glass of bubbles over lunch and talk about the business all at the same time.

Having read her book now, I was pleasantly surprised and called to tell her after I read the last chapter, that despite her concerns, it was VERY good.

Karen's words, "If people can just take something away from this book and apply in their everyday life, I have achieved my goal of reaching out to help people to feel whole again." I agreed if you can get a takeaway or two from a book – something that you remember and that resonates with you, then you are doing well, and I feel Karen has definitely achieved that. EnJOY.

Karen Vercoe
Business Partner and Long-term friend

Preface

I had not realised I had a book in me until I allowed myself to dig deep. I knew I loved inspiring others and spent many hours writing prolific quotes and short stories. I even created a business called WritBitz (writing bits n pieces), creating journals to share in the world.

I am inspired every day by my husband who loves and supports me whilst allowing me to be my own person. My gorgeous sons who are alongside cheering me on.

My son Dylan with his physical disabilities brought me back to my heart knowing that no matter what life throws at us we can rise to the challenge and see it merely as an opportunity to grow as a person.

'Life is a journey' became my new mantra and my new norm. I had a new set of priorities. One was to make it about me, and then secondly how that can transpire to help others in a similar situation to feel complete, to live an awe-inspired life that they leap out of bed each day, or to feel a sense of peace in their lives.

I have had many aha moments, not believing in myself and nearly giving up on myself. I shed many tears throughout my life, but so many more writing this book as I peel back the layers to recover my natural state of being.

We often have little control over things that happen to us in life: the death of a loved one, illness, losing jobs, breakups, war, poverty, abuse. However, we can control how we respond and react when these things happen.

My focus daily now is that life is a journey, it is simply to take back control of our lives, to lend a hand, to give comfort, and just like a morning cup of tea, not having to prove anything.

I travelled overseas as part of this book getting back to my roots to bring something to the world that has meaning. The meaning of life.

Table of Contents

Foreword vii
Preface ix
Introduction 1
1: The Journey to Self-Love 7
2: Inner Fulfilment 21
3: Knowing There Is More Out There 35
4: Be Yourself 49
5: Lost Identity 63
6: Wearing A Mask For The World 75
7: Surviving to Thriving 89
8: Finding Your Joy 103
9: Stand In Your Own Power 117
10: Create The Life You Desire 131
Conclusion 145
Acknowledgements 147
About The Author 149

Introduction

*You may not control all the events that happen to you.
But you can decide not to be reduced by them.*

Maya Angelou

A frightened wounded little girl striving to find her feet in the wilderness of life without direction, love, or guidance. Struck with abandonment and feeling alone.

The self-actualisation, the opening up to face the pain, and having that moment to understand, to know love. How this can paralyse you and how the feeling it leaves you is the same for many people, just a different story running.

People disappear all the time, disappearances after all have explanations, usually. Strange the things you remember, single images and experiences that stay with you for years. Abandonment can feel raw and painful, just like trauma.

When someone is abandoned, that painful experience can stay with them through life and be easily triggered. I know as that was me. When it does get triggered, it floods you with fear, panic, and intense shame.

The secret, once you understand your story from your childhood, mine to be, that as a child in the early years were spent disconnected from the world because there was too much pain being connected with those I was meant to love.

I experienced abandonment by my mother. My father was unable to show love only anger. Isolation became my new best friend, and my absence was present. I literally ran and hid from the world.

Somehow in my mind, I can still recall the detail of that day to hear the words "your mother has left us."

I often wondered if I belonged to this world, was there a way out? I do know this, even now after all the pain and heartbreak that followed, however at times feeling very much the stranger in a strange land, I wouldn't change a thing.

Sometimes you find yourself on a path you never expected.

My experiences left me feeling I was not good enough, I was nothing special, I was unattractive, or I was too young, and being controlled by societies acceptance.

My life was being controlled like a video game because I was constantly trying to seek the approval of everyone around me.

What I thought was the way to impress my peers and gain the approval of everyone around me was killing me slowly. It was tearing me away from what true success was and what true happiness is. Being happy an odd sensation. A beginning perhaps.

It is like a double-edged sword. (My desire to please others) got me up and it got me moving, learning new ways, to always push myself, and to understand myself on a completely new level. But after being on such a good high, feeling great, knowing I was looking great, it took just a simple few words or negativity to bring me down.

I was finally ready to accept and to feel that at a very early age my child self was abandoned and wounded deeply. I was determined now to know this in my body, my mind, my heart. I decided to take an inward journey, to heal my past in the present.

The deep inner work felt like an awakening. I have experienced pain, fear, excitement, pleasure, loss, anger, power, sadness, clarity, understanding, love. I have felt young, fragile, wounded, wise, brave, strong, proud. I have tapped into buried emotions and connections, years of denial and confusion now leading into insight and clarity.

You cannot change your life unless you go inward and find your own wisdom. Believe it and follow it. Be what you said you would when you came into this life. Talk in a patient way, like you said you would.

Your life was destined to be great however we get lost in the confusion and the people around us are not going to always have your best interest at heart.

The journey I took last year began with a strong desire to know, to feel, to heal. Soon after this intention was declared, my "journey" took on a life of its own.

My trauma did not make me who I am today my resilience did. I won't ever credit those that tried to break me, as all credit goes to my ability to remove pieces that should never have been and find ways to rebuild.

I hope you enjoy reading my story and that it contributes to the change you are wanting more than anything.

You aren't just good enough you are Great! Guard your bodies and the precious miracle of your own life. Know your greatness always.

To love yourself means your cup will be overflowing

Chapter 1
The Journey to Self-Love

"Love recognises no barriers, its jumps hurdles, leaps fences, penetrates walls to arrive at its destination full of hope."

Maya Angelou

Turning back time to 1962

As I revisit my life tears are streaming down my face uncontrollably even knowing that my heart can't really break it feels like it's doing exactly that.

Turning back the clock to 3rd July 1962 where it all began. I was born into a family that was living outside of what society would call a healthy family system. We were poor, we lived with my grandparents, my father could not show love. He married my mother which could be referred to as a 'shotgun wedding'. My mother who now sits in an aged care facility, when asked what is one of her biggest regrets, it was marrying my father.

Karen (the accident) emerges into the world after a healthy pregnancy, reasonable 8hour labour, and acceptable birth. So, everything seemed just perfect. The description from my mother was I was very big, a mop of red hair, and rather squashed from going full term with little room to move at the end before my journey into the world.

The person pacing the floor rather impatiently was my father calling every 15mins during the labour asking if I had arrived as they weren't allowed in the birthing suite. I can only imagine now being a mother myself and being his first child meant he would be excited & anxious all at the same time. What was life going to be like, and was he ready for this responsibility? Finally, after driving the midwives crazy he was allowed in to witness his first, and what turned out to be his only natural child.

In the day, we were placed in cribs behind a large glass window on display for all parents to witness their creation for the very first time. My father approached the window looking for me. However, it seemed the first 30 seconds of my life was the most important to him, and I was definitely not what he had expected or built up in his own mind.

Hold this thought for a moment and feel for my mother who only moments before endured childbirth. So that moment of holding a child for the first time, quite often labour has all but been forgotten. It has not really been forgotten, but the happiness and reward colour the memory of the preceding pain.

The moment that changed my life forever

My father hurried to my mother's bedside and blurted out, then regurgitated at every family event following, the words were recalled very specifically, "Oh Ann, 'isn't she ugly, what are we going to do."

I think everything is made worse, because, at the core of your life, the very people who should be making you feel good about yourself are doing the opposite. It is wrong of your parents to say those things, not good parenting, however just because your parents are saying it, doesn't make it the truth. I look back and think the fact they were like this meant they were very unhappy with themselves.

When people (such as your parents) don't like who they are inside, they find it easier to project how they feel on to others to try to get rid of that feeling, instead of looking at themselves and thinking, "How can I work on myself?"

Life over my informative years was like one big party. Every weekend generally at someone's home was loud music, much alcohol consumed, people sleeping with other partners, and all the time we were sent to bed and told to be quiet, in fact, words that I can recall being used were "shut that bitch up."

Lots of alcohol-fuelled arguments became my new normal.

I had dismissed thinking or feeling much of anything really, I became numb. I would cry myself to sleep, in fact, I cried all the time. I didn't have the experience or voice to change things, so I just retreated. I couldn't run away I was only a child. So, I just got on with life and built walls around myself as protection and became a survivor.

I was a Survivor and became very good at it

I spent the next 50 years of my life thinking I was ugly. The ugly duckling who didn't get the boyfriends, who admired girls afar who were seemingly attractive, and I just desperately wanted to be them, anyone but myself.

The story running in my head I wasn't good enough started from the minute I was born and set in stone for life.

I felt a calling to tell my story in the hope that I can help others realise life doesn't happen to us, it happens for us. We can change our reality at any time given the right tools. What we have inside of us is not necessarily our story.

As I share my story, I soon came to realise that everyone had their own story running with a different spin, but the same ending left the overall feeling of emptiness.

The secret is how we go from where we are feeling stuck or restricted to feeling free and happy. Remove the shackles that we ourselves placed.

I was lost never to be found

After eight years of living in the UK, our family decided they would move to another country on the other side of the world, to improve our current lifestyle. So off we went on our big adventure to Australia the chosen country for a better life we were told.

The cracks returned and the reasons for leaving England were still there in fact because of the lifestyle in Australia parties became a regular thing as well as hangovers. Love was absent and the arguments got worse.

Love does a lot for a human being, that deeper connection. Once felt its magical...powerful... force for healing. It reunites the ununited, opens the mind, 'fixes' the seemingly broken, and encourages those who feel they have no hope. It breathes life where there is no life.

> "The first step towards getting somewhere, is to decide you are not going to stay where you are."
>
> **JP Morgan**

How did I become so lost?

I had an eventful young life, to say the least. I don't know how others saw me, but in my mind, I was a nutty, self-conscious, rather lost little girl from the UK looking to fit in. I know I'm not that same little girl and that life is more beautiful and meaningful than I ever thought possible.

In saying that, I'm also not exactly where I thought I'd be at this time in my life either. Which is perfectly fine. Because I know I am where I'm meant to be, and that I still have time to become all that I want to be too.

As mentioned earlier in the introduction whilst on my path to self-love journey my trauma didn't make me who I am today, my resilience and the action I took did. I won't ever credit those that tried to break me, all credit goes to my ability to remove pieces that should never have been and finding ways to rebuild.

It is up to you, the energy spent casting blame for how you are feeling is only going to affect you.

This played out in so many ways throughout my life. I fell victim to narcissistic girls at school. I spent my early years always wanting to fit in with the cool group rather than the people that mattered most which I hadn't even considered.

I did not understand why people were kind one day and particularly unkind the next. I was kind to people and hurt easily so this was like have the big sign on my forehead 'L' for Loser. I had no self-worth or self-love I was running on empty. I was a lost little girl living outside my body, constantly seeking love and confirmation externally.

Being outside of my physical body took a lot of energy. I had no identity I was just surviving without the foundations, instability and resentment was something that I could relate to.

Without solid foundations meant any struggles I would feel the force behind them tipping me over easily, and upside down creating more sadness in my life. My foundations were built on sand, rather than rock-solid.

I wasn't even able to make decisions for myself. If I heard that someone had done something bad, or unforgivable then I would consider that gospel and carried angst inside of me which overtime layer upon layer consumed me that I didn't know which way was up. Who was right & who was wrong?

I listened to others rather than myself always not forming my own opinion. I felt stuck and unable to make decisions with no knowledge, emotional intelligence or experience to deal with anything that came my way. I was a victim of my own circumstances. You look up to your parents, teachers and authorities, and believe everything you hear to be true.

Now where I stand looking from a completely different perspective, I can confidently say you will not always feel like this, I promise. How you feel will change because as you get older and leave home, you will choose who to surround yourself with, and they are likely to be people who make you feel good.

You will start to see yourself differently and understand that, like all of us, you have bits that are unique to you, and although you might not be "perfect", in time you will learn to like yourself.

I'm not promising you won't ever meet nasty people, but you will get better at coping and understanding that the problem comes from them, not you. Plus, it won't matter so much, because they won't be your parents and you won't be living with them, having your self-esteem constantly eroded.

In my early 20s I moved away from my family (parents) as I knew they would continue to control my life if I allowed it, and I did. I had my brothers living in Townsville North Queensland, so it made sense to move somewhere where I knew people to get started, or so I thought.

My first experience living away from home and in a shared arrangement was a narcissist woman and I didn't see this coming. Can you see the pattern? I hadn't dealt with my issues so still wherever I turned up I was faced with the same people. The survival mode kicked in and I knew this was time for me to stand on my own two feet, own my crap and take some action to change.

Sounds easy right? I needed to identify the areas in my life that needed the work so as you can imagine I fumbled along a little longer playing the victim.

Once I did realise the importance of taking ownership and responsibility for the crap in my life, and to take control (take the reins), I could start to move forward.

I was always a dedicated reader but didn't discriminate. Someone offered me Louise Hayes inspirational books which was the beginning to shifting my mindset. Quite quickly my library became flooded with personal development, anything I could get my hands on to break through this feeling of being stuck and always seeking something or that someone.

We will always be on our path in learning and growing as this is a journey, your life journey, but we can make it easier for ourselves.

Remember every moment is an opportunity to change the way you think or feel about something, someone or a situation.

Don't waste time playing the blame game or getting angry at those who don't want or need the same things you do. Don't wait for them to come on board, or help you get what you want. Don't try to fix them to fit you.

You have your own business to get on with, learning to stay in your own business is the best-kept secret. Get busy taking care of what is important to you by you.

My husband and I had a child late in life who has multiple disabilities we had our usual ups and downs as a couple however our relationship was solid, our love was the forever stuff. We had a great partnership to allow our son to thrive not just survive.

We also had our own needs to be fulfilled which over time we were able to achieve. He wrote and recorded songs, and I was writing this book. It is about balance in all aspects of life.

It took a while for me to get to where I am today, as for many years I would look at attractive girls and want to be them, instead of feeling attractive, as we need to remember everyone's perception is different. I had already decided I was unattractive so everything we have heard or learned behaviours are more difficult to change however you can change, it works as I am living proof.

I would want my partner to tell me I am attractive, or you look great in that outfit. However, I could never compliment myself so how did I propose that was going to work. We need to think of ourselves as magnets we attract the same type of feelings and thoughts.

I got to the stage where I would out loud ask questions of myself to wait for an answer and you know it works. Sometimes I questioned the answer, ha-ha we sabotage ourselves all the time.

I kept this up and I started creating my own future and discriminated what I wanted in my life, not influenced by anyone about what I should do, be and have.

Many things in this world we cannot explain. I knew I could no longer wait for permission for love to find me. I had found two possible escape routes one to freedom, and the other finding love.

Daily habits to reclaim your life

(grab a pen and paper). The pen is still mightier than a keyboard. You are directing movement by thought when writing.

First things first, grab a mirror and repeat after me. "I love you; I have always loved you; you are the love of my life." (at least 12 times every day)

Main purpose statement - Create your own main purpose statements using your aspirations, hold them in your heart, and say it as if they already exist in your life.

It will be a challenge as we are so conditioned to think I don't deserve that, or how can I afford, or have those things in my life, only the rich and famous have those things, or whatever the negative thoughts that show up for you.

It's been proven that it is easier to think something negative, rather than create a positive thought.

It really is about creating new behaviours, habits, which for many don't know they exist.

It's the old saying you don't know what you don't know. The only way we can change is by not doing the same thing and expecting different results.

Journaling – I began journaling, in the beginning, to bring life to my thoughts. Somehow seeing them on paper allows you to witness your thoughts in 3D.

Scribble it out using the exact emotion you are feeling, anger, sadness, happy, then read it, and decide if this is, or is not serving you anymore.

In most cases, it won't be, so we take this opportunity that has presented itself to say thank you to that thought and let it go on its merry way.

As you write listen to the words you are using. For example, if you say, I want stability in my life, it could mean you are feeling unstable. Acknowledging this is the beginning and keep going, dig deep. Many have lived an unstable life within their family unit, so they are seeking stability, and don't have the tools, however acknowledging it is the beginning to overcoming it.

Get comfortable with being uncomfortable.

People Pleasers – My pet hate are people-pleasers. This does nothing for a person's soul as generally in my experience, people-pleasers then expect that you will do the same for them.

It doesn't work that way we need to be who we are and allow others to do the same. It's called respect. If it doesn't suit that other person, then just walk away as they will suck your energy. Hang with those that align with you.

Disconnection – We talked about disconnection which I spent much of my life being. For me, I needed to be connected to find peace in my life. For many, the connection is the key, and as you are reading this most likely you feel like you are disconnected at times.

I also needed to know what being 'connected' meant. I have brought my story to the beginning of my life as the disconnection started from day one.

I needed to bring a story to you which meant every fibre of my being was shared in my life that I thought was a struggle. Don't be the person in the aged care facility at 90 with regrets. Follow your calling.

Blaming – When you hear yourself going into a blame game, whether against other people, the world, life, whomever… say "stop" to yourself out loud, and actually, turn your attention away from your blaming thoughts. Acknowledge them and move on.

Think about the things that are driving you to distraction in your life, the things you feel you wanted, and then when you got them, the feeling of emptiness was still there, you then turned your attention to something else, and so on so that you never felt a sense of peace.

Be the change you want to see in the world.

Mahatma Gandhi

Each time you didn't feel complete because you were not the driver of them, you were just the expression of them from your childhood. Those drivers that were learned behaviours from the people you looked up to. These are beliefs and have set us up for life.

You can change your reality anytime you want. Also, you can have your cake and eat it too.

Remove your shoes and feel the earth under your feet, or with your hands. Think about it as a kid we loved playing in the dirt and there's a reason for that getting back to nature where we belong. We need to be connected to the earth. Play in the dirt, sand anything bringing you a connection with mother nature.

Allow laughter in your life, so big belly laughs, just laugh and just allow it to consume you.

Simple joy despite my eagerness to leave a small part of me regretted the imminent escape I still needed to find distractions for my ever-present darkness.

To love yourself means your cup will be overflowing, to be in a space only ever coming from love means you can share your gifts to the world ...and in return the hearts of those who love you will humble you.

We never want to dismiss our past or what we felt caused us grief as you could reference these feelings if you want to, thoughts as a growing pain.

We all get to experience it and are grateful as to what got us to where we are today. Of the many things that cross our path in life, so many of them still truly matters.

Do not give away your control to others, own it

Chapter 2
Inner Fulfilment

Karen Howe

I do my best because I'm counting on you counting on me.

Maya Angelou

Nothing changes until you do

I spent time comparing myself, seeking love and approval of others, I tried really hard and got very good at it, explored enough of it, and failed enough to find the one thing, I was still miserable.

A phrase that I recall as a teen was "compare or despair," because no matter what you are comparing can be guaranteed you will feel bad or empty in the end. I reminded myself, I was not an adequate judge of my own abilities, so stop comparing, and start just doing your best and what feels right.

The only way you can live a happy and fulfilled life is to live it to the fullest one day at a time.

By not taking responsibility for ourselves we give away our control to others. Happy and fulfilled people take back that control from other people. They take back responsibility for their lives. They make their own choices and their own decisions.

They take action and live the life they want, not based on other's opinions. If you want to be happier and more fulfilled, know where you want to be. Don't allow anyone or anything to stop you from pursuing your purpose.

Set your own path and define your own success. Do not pattern your life after other people's lives. Only you can live your life for yourself.

We did some travelling in our caravan for 10+ weeks around parts of Australia. Without realising we didn't watch any form of TV or listen to the world news. We, my lifelong partner (husband extraordinaire) and myself decided we needed to get back to mother nature, particularly for our son who struggles with his disabilities. His sensory issues meant school was challenging for him, so we needed to remove him from the classroom.

We needed to get back to basics and put everything into perspective as our lives during the last 10+ years had been uncertain. We didn't know what our son's life was going to look like, and everything that was happening at the time, just seemed to be happening to us, and I was spiralling out of control. We had nothing to lose as we were striving for a more fulfilled life.

I called this trip my lifesaver, my turning point in life for massive change, and opportunity towards inner fulfilment.

No-one makes an impact by trying to fit in and follow the norm. It is breaking the mould that we discover there is no one else like us and that's what makes us unique and itself is wonderful.

Cherish all that makes you, you and only you get to experience the depth of meaning to your life. You will wonder what took you so long.

I am not exactly where I thought I'd be at this time in my life. Which is perfectly fine. Because I know I am where I'm meant to be, and that I still have time to become all that I want to be whilst on this journey.

Seeing the bigger picture to fulfilment

Acknowledge everything in life, the detail, and most importantly understand whatever we do, we need to be accountable for our own actions, and can no longer cast blame. When you get to this level of self-awareness you start to feel lighter like a feather floating through life. Never placing any expectations on self, or seeking confirmation, just supporting each other is the best gift in life to each other.

Time passes, fast forward and at 57 years old I now find myself on a high more often and unable to shake my high. I was no longer trying to be someone else or trying to fit in, I was just simply me. I was no longer trying to get somewhere I was already there.

People think addicts love drugs. Wrong. Addicts love anything that keeps them distracted from loving themselves or the feeling of fulfilment.

When you love your life, and it feels on track, you want to keep heading in this direction. Because you are enjoying the process and excited to see what else it will bring.

You will hit roadblocks as growth or change is inevitable as we can't stay the same and be healthy and happy. It does require action and understanding of that you are seeking in life. Sometimes it just means time to pause.

I looked at the areas in my life I wanted to change and decided to do just that.

One was to take back control of my own life and own it, and then write a book about it.

You don't need to focus on becoming "better". Instead, you simply do things because you value them, because you love the process, and appreciate every moment as if it is your last. Like a child each experience becomes exciting.

You won't always strive to 'get better', but instead will grow naturally

You are already perfect. And it is true. There is no destination, you are already there.

There is simply a journey to be enjoyed.

Just as a seed is as perfect as the tree it becomes you can be happy with yourself and your life at all stages of development. For all of life's stages are just different forms of this one greatness.

When we stop rating (comparing) the world around us and getting annoyed whenever it didn't live up to any expectation, that feeling we have of what may happen and put our interpretation on this is our greatest trap in life.

Imagine if we just allowed ourselves to grow and expand, overtime your energy will increase and opportunities will be presented to you by keeping an open mind.

What if we remain open to receiving things we desire, in a sense remove any expectations? Expectations place conditions in the world, myself, my life. Instead, simply let everything be just as nature intended. Be in the flow.

During the process discovering one of the greatest insights of all when you are open to the world and no longer try to cage it by expecting it to fulfil your limited view of perfection, its true beauty is revealed. That life is about uncovering the greatness which already exists.

Just a side note, with these changes come some natural fallouts with either friends or family. Nothing you have said, or done, however, it stirs up the demons in many. Quite often it can be time to let go of that thing or person.

You might say I'm excited and ready for a change which is why you are reading this book as by no coincidence. How did I get here, and how do I find my way back to who I am, not who you were conditioned to be?

Not everyone will get you and that's okay

One thing I do understand now is the experiences that caused so much pain for me was pivotal that it permitted me to allow me to get to a place of awakening. Maybe you have become stronger or you now see things differently and you can't always pinpoint it you just notice the changes that make you feel better.

Create life like a game. My experience was I was ugly which turned into unattractive and lacking connection, but now I am aware of this it enabled me to identify the gaps in my life. I was from a disconnected family and I was avoiding connection with others.

Once I felt connected and to do this was painful at first, putting myself out there meeting new people and sharing my story, and bit by bit I realised I had something to offer, and it wasn't about sitting back waiting it was about getting out there and doing it over and over.

Many will be afraid to take the leap of faith to grow and expand and recognise areas in their lives that potentially are holding them back or create new things to improve their lives.

Many do not realise there is more to be had because if you don't have anything to strive for, you don't know it exists, or you may feel you don't deserve a life of fulfilment, and the only people happy are those with things and money.

It requires consistency and commitment, and once you know or feel there is more out there waiting for you, which by the way if you don't make that change you are denying the world of your gift. Please don't do that.

Remember life is a journey and you never reach a destination however you will reach some awesome people and opportunities once you allow them. This is life-changing when realising you are here to serve others and help them be that change contributing to a peaceful harmonious world. Who doesn't want that?

"The first step towards getting somewhere, is to decide you are not going to stay where you are."

JP Morgan

First steps to fulfilment

The first step is to not take on all the sadness in the world in a way that is not helpful. Being helpful is offering your services or financial assistance or just listening. We can't fix the world and why worry about what we can't change.

Turn off the TV and STOP absorbing the news, the sad stuff. I don't mean close yourself off however the media sensationalise everything you will never seek the truth. Instead, select a program that provides you with highlights and minimise the drama that is in our faces each and every day. Drama drains us.

Inner fulfilment an inside job

So, I heard this term, love is an inside job, or happiness an inside job. The question for me was, but how do I go about finding it? As soon as I asked the question the answer popped up, sit with yourself and allow your feelings to surface.

Just keep asking questions until you start getting in the flow. Buyer beware once you start this there is no turning back as the feeling is going to propel you toward more and more inner fulfilment.

When I started writing this book I had no idea what I was going to write contextually, and even if I could write a book, I was still working on my self during this time so what I am bringing to you is direct from the heart, and has been over a year in the making however a lifetime in the planning.

I knew I wanted to bring my gift to the world and that gift of releasing my fears or those things that were restricting my life in the hope that others will begin to feel the same sense of freedom.

I was enjoying taking time for myself to enable me to open myself up to the world you could say wakeup Karen. I was in the zone which can be described as being in the flow, then the words began to flow.

Fear of not being good enough or who would want to read my book and worry about what will people think of me. I did much travel and research during this time. I am blessed with a partner who gifted me this opportunity as he knew what I was capable of even before I knew. He could see my gift for that alone I am grateful.

The old saying treat people the way you would like to be treated. Not feel the need to seek love, as remember love is an inside job. Wholehearted loving begins with a *choice, commitment, celebration, compassion, co-creation and courage.*

A chief component of a healthy relationship with self is recognising that our every act be it physical, financial, sexual, spiritual, and emotional involves a choice, even when we imagine ourselves to be helpless.

Only when we feel capable of living well on our own can we choose to live freely and fully. The same as being able to say yes to a relationship with a whole heart, we need to know we can also say no and thrive on our own. We're the leaders of our own lives.

When we are committed to self, our participation in the relationship is unqualified. We mean to stick around for the entire ride, not just to enjoy the side trip of love. We promise ourselves that we will work hard to enrich and deepen the relationship within, which includes taking the time to make it a priority.

Commitment also involves an honest examination of the limitations that make love and collaboration with self and others in our lives challenging. Commitment includes a pledge to self that we will do the inside work necessary to make the relationship with ourselves flourish.

All spiritual traditions emphasise that each person has his or her own calling and that to discover and celebrate is our life's work.

Note: Compassion is not the same as indulgence. We can maintain clear boundaries and honour our needs for safety and accountability, even while understanding each other's struggles and vulnerabilities.

We can stretch to see conflicts from the other's perspective rather than remaining mirrored in our own point of view. We can make the effort to cultivate an interest in each other rather than passing judgment, and to respond with openheartedness even when our instinct is to close up like a clam.

We can forgive ourselves and forgive others, again and again. Our stumbles are as much a part of the journey as our successes.

One of the most powerful skills we can develop is the shared creation of effective ways to manage conflict, communicate, share decisions, and support each other in difficult times.

Cocreation can also involve the pursuit of common interests that extend the relationship beyond its customary "you-me" borders. It's healthy to broaden your life, be it through family or community connections, creative projects, intellectual pursuits, sports, music, travel, spiritual practice, friendships, or other endeavours that you find rewarding. Joint endeavours can create larger meaning in our relationships.

Bravery is necessary for moving forward. We need the courage to confront ourselves with awareness, honesty, and love. Courage means facing our fears and limitations. It involves challenging our expectations and assumptions about others, about who they should and should not be.

It means making changes when they are called for. It is feeling compassion for the whole of our human condition — mine, yours, that of our families, and even of people we feel have wronged us. Bravery is finding a way to laugh at ourselves, too.

Daily habits to reclaim your life

I love sharing with you the elements of my daily success routine and see if the pieces might help you create your own routine for inner fulfilment!

Write down what you believe your gift is, what motivates you today and every day. What gets you out of bed feeling energised if you could do that thing every day.

Don't be afraid to try new habits and see how they work for you. If they leave you feeling energised and inspired, keep doing them…if they don't keep trying new ones until you find ones that do.

Learn to pay attention to what works, discover small rituals of connection, and find times and ways to play and make the type of love that you can integrate into your everyday lives.

Always remind yourself that your primary job is to find your own unique purpose and fulfil it. Creating new habits and stacking them will create an opening toward this.

"Good habits are hard to form but easy to live with. Bad habits are easy to form but hard to live with."

Brian Tracy

Each of us struggles with the human condition, and we must extend compassion to others.

Tell someone how you feel, be kind to yourself. Know that what you project you are feeling within you. You may need to feel uncomfortable with this. The new comfortable is being uncomfortable as without it we won't grow. It is all about stretching ourselves beyond what we know right now.

"Hi, you are looking amazing today, I just wanted to tell you that."

The people who come into our lives enrich and challenge us. Through these relationships, we can see ourselves more clearly. The health of our connections with one another depends a great deal on what goes on inside us — our inner resources, our lingering demons, and our motivation to grow and change.

As good as a relationship can be, our emotional and spiritual life journey begins and ends within us. In this sense, every relationship is an inside job. Inside us is where it starts — and where it finishes, too.

Problem blindness means you cannot see a problem so you can't solve it

Chapter 3

Knowing There Is More Out There

If you are always trying to be normal you will never know how amazing you can be

Maya Angelou

The rest of the world has a right to know

You have dreams, goals, and this idea of who you are supposed to be, but you don't feel like you're living up to any of them.

I was constantly asking myself, "Is this it? I feel there is more to life than just existing or surviving as I refer to it? Want to know what made things even worse? I was "successful" in the eyes of a lot of people. I felt guilty for even playing with the idea that my life was unfulfilled.

You can close your eyes to the things you don't want to see, but you can't close your heart to the things you don't want to feel.

Johnny Depp

I couldn't keep pretending that everything was okay. In my heart, I knew something was missing, although I didn't know exactly what that was, or what my next steps were. I was the frightened little girl seeking love, and to be accepted. I was blinded by the problem and seemed all too consuming.

Problem blindness assumes that the problem is natural or inevitable, and there's nothing you can do about it. And we shrug it off. "That's just the way it is," we decide. So, we don't try. When we don't see a problem, we can't solve it. And that blindness can create passivity even in the face of enormous harm.

I continued talking to myself more, yes got very good at this and sometimes telling myself off, and asking questions out loud with every answer that came, was an opportunity to journal each of these uncomfortable feelings that showed up, speaking outwardly bit by bit clearing my jumbled mind.

Years of sadness just came pouring out, crying was normal to me, and the feeling of hopelessness.

My family would say, "oh really, what are you crying about now?" "Karen cried her life away I'm surprised she hasn't drowned in her own tears." I think about the life that was presented to me and now understand through my family's disconnection I never felt safe, just pure sadness, and not because I was a sook or cry baby, but because I was surrounded in a life of misery.

The more I spoke out and began to understand that I was living a life that had no depth to it, I was starting to find I wanted to discover more about who I am and what am I here to do.

I kept on this mission which consumed me as every corner I turned, I began to realise how much more I could achieve, and attract in my life, and how the cloud was slowly lifting.

I came across this piece which resonated with me. "We live in a downstream world. We can have a bias for downstream action. We can spend most of our time reacting to problems downstream rather than dealing with the source of the problem that is found upstream."

I had a knowing that change was inevitable, and I have control over what I think, say, and do, and that I have always had this control around my life. Once I had concluded that I had surrendered my control to the government (i.e. parents, authorities, family, friends) I could think for myself.

The frightened little girl living inside a woman's body, and it was time to grow up. Stop focussing on the past, or the future and look at where I am at right now. Focus on the good that is happening now.

We're either too busy reminiscing about the past or thinking about the future to appreciate all the wonderful things that are happening right now.

I made it about me

Make it about you first and then everything falls into place. Make sure your cup is overflowing, so it can flow on to the next thing or person where you want to make a difference.

Overtime fear was leaving me, in fact I was speaking out about who I am and understanding my uniqueness, and how

I could make a difference in the world which also helped trace steps to the root cause.

In the years that followed, I learnt to create a life filled with a crazy deep sense of purpose, sustainable happiness, and getting paid to do work I love while making a meaningful impact in the world.

My passion for writing returned which we have in all of us even if journaling daily a great way of healing.

Writing was an opportunity to discover the depth of my character, the depth of love, commitment, patience, and abilities; the opportunity to explore my spirit more deeply than I could have imagined possible. My son drove me further than I would ever go on my own, working harder, seeking answers to many questions.

I continued this exercise of writing for every bout of crying and outburst. I just kept drilling down as to why I was feeling so much emotion for everything that would show up in my thoughts. I worked at this daily and consistency was the key to achieving the result of coming out of life as the victim.

After a few more decades there was a knowing that brought one woman to trust again. A knowing that guided a woman to protect her child who also was 9 at the time from those who on the surface appeared loving and safe.

I do believe we have stories inside us all. Stories that perhaps we have never told because they are too difficult for us to accept as true, or being judged from telling the truth, or where someone or something appears in our lives unexpectedly and challenges our held beliefs.

Then we start to question and are no longer confident we operate solely with our five senses to manoeuvre through life. There is something more trying to surface from within.

Playing the role of the therapist when you are the victim is almost an unthinkable task, however my end goal was clear, as I wanted to be the happy person and be able to love again.

Consider the unlimited possibilities

Consider the possibility there is a divine knowing available to us, and all that is required on our part is to open to it. Much of this for me showed up within three years after our son was born as I questioned my very existence as I grew up feeling different and now Dylan was going to experience the same. Not sure I can face the staring and the questions.

I laugh at myself every time I think back about those thoughts, how limiting it was to even think that way. I then forgave myself as I knew I was coming from the unconscious mind (auto pilot) not the conscious mind (awareness/depth). Once I had the tools to be aware of my conscious thoughts it was then I realised he gifted me this opportunity, an opportunity to change how the world viewed us.

> "Until you make the unconscious conscious, it will direct your life and you will call it fate."
>
> **Carl Jung**

Now being more confident and happier I feel I can write and share with others offering messages of hope and what is our god given birth right to live an extraordinary life, not just exist,

NO, a life filled with things much bigger than you. Remember we are born to thrive not just survive.

Asking for help was the biggest challenge for me. Communicating openly with the closest person is the key, and I owe a lot to my husband who was that person in terms of allowing me to do what I needed to do to claw my way back to finding my truth and what my role on planet earth was.

This was the work that took much discipline and took much resistance to not go back to the old ways, and if I did, I would catch myself doing it.

I found I wasn't angry at the world anymore, and my energy lifted, and I was leaving the negativity behind me. Out of all my journaling, one of the things I had lost along the way was my writing as a child I loved the written word.

Throughout my book, I talk about my experiences, in many cases after hearing many other stories, whilst the stories may differ the feelings you are left with are the same, unfulfilled, unhappy, empty, lonely and the list goes on.

Our emotions are an important aspect of our experience of ourselves and our quality of life, yet most of us have some degree of trouble allowing ourselves to have certain feelings.

I believe that the more attention we give to this knowing energy around us, the more we will feel the abundance of life and be less likely to think, "Is this all there is and avoid seeking what we feel we are missing outside of ourselves?"

Fortunately, two things are true, you have time to get on track, and you are probably not as far off as you think. Share your story to all who will listen, our storytelling will inspire others to bring forth experiences deep within them too.

Sharing our stories can warm our hearts, bring excitement to the moment, and enlarge the connectedness we all have to one another. Great stories can happen to those that can tell them.

You have the ability, to focus on what matters and control your thoughts and actions.

So, my first marriage was into the Chinese culture and way of life thinking they are very family-oriented as that was what I was seeking. However, doesn't matter about the culture I soon worked out I needed to accept responsibility and be in control of my own life and my own business.

'Family' is one of my highest values. It required much work and energy and a very patient husband for me to feel the love again. The strange part about all of this is I knew I loved my family, but I didn't know how to express my love.

This came from my father so the chain needed to be broken and then healed so I could move on.

You can't blame anyone or anything for how your life turns out however you can focus on, and build on, becoming that person you want to be. That was a choice I made to feel again which required change.

"Change is the law of life. And those who look only to the past or the present are certain to miss the future"

John F Kennedy

We are surrounded by change and it is the one thing that has the most dramatic impact on our lives. There is no avoiding change as it will find you, challenge you and force you to reconsider how to live your life.

> *"Your life does not get better by chance; it gets better by change."*
>
> **Jim Rohn**

Remember every situation is an opportunity to change the way you think about something. Don't waste time and energy blaming or passing the buck to those who don't want or need the same things you do, don't wait for them to come on board or help you get what you want.

Name it, and do what you need to do to, so make it happen — for yourself. Practice saying "No." If you don't want to do something, and only doing it to please someone, don't do it. Remember that you have needs, just like everyone does.

Every single one of us has a unique reason why we are here walking, talking, doing. Ask what it is you are here to do? If it seems unimaginable keep dreaming until you get there to do it just like me writing this book was unimaginable, but I just gave myself a kick in the ass and stuck with it.

There will always be naysayers, however for me to move forward I needed to do this to expand my dialogue, my feelings, my energy. I was busting to get this out there to share that once I was a victim, I was bullied, then became the bully, and then took responsibility for my own actions owned my own crap.

Description of a victim is a person who has come to feel helpless and passive in the face of misfortune and ill-treatment.

Daily habits to reclaim your life

Rinse and repeat previous habits as they have become your new normal. You will work out what works for you and as long as you establish that and apply it you will be kicking goals.

"For the past 33 years, I have looked in the mirror every morning and asked myself: "If today were the last day of my life, would I want to do what I am about to do today?" And whenever the answer has been "No" for too many days in a row, I know I need to change something."

Steve Jobs

Decide to never walk in anyone's shadow. Which means saying 'No' when you are urged to say 'Yes' to please someone.

Reading and absorbing as much information that will lead you to growth in your personal development. Anything to feed your brain with nourishing information all the while journaling your thoughts.

My new qualification became 'Life experiences' (life skills) which will serve us far greater than a Degree. First, you must have your foundations set in stone, not sand.

Get more curious about the world If you've managed to retain some of the curiosity you had as a child. If the world hasn't beaten it out of you yet, hold onto it for dear life and explore your options sooner rather than later.

Deep down in the very core of you, you know that you can have more in your life.

You know that short-term pleasure and long-term joy are two fundamentally different outcomes.

Once you've begun succeeding at any endeavour, you'll reach a threshold where you must decide if you're ready to go to the next level. Most people get comfortable at a certain stage because they don't want to deal with the emotional purging involved in up levelling as it involves change.

It's about knowing when change is coming, when it is the right time to step up with the least resistance, the next phase of growth as nothing ever stays the same.

If you want to go from ordinary to extraordinary you need to change what you are doing and then you will reach that next level, you will have a few growing pains but you will see the changes will begin to enhance your life. You will wake up more invigorated and excited.

Just like going to the gym, you experience a natural treatment as movement is very important for us, but we do get excited after a period when you see results.

It won't be long until you get your stride back. But this time you'll be more evolved. More able. The stakes will be higher. You'll have more help and support. Everything will mean more. It is to give up ideas of what you think you are meant to do or be and surrender any reasons you think can't or won't happen.

To work with anxiety and other emotions - Do grounding exercise, walk in nature, limit the amount of news/social media/take a magnesium supplement, focus on deep breaths.

Drink more water and take long baths, rest, journal, do yoga, wear loose clothing and slow down. Go with the flow.

Avoid the trap of validation

As a baby, we need love and to know we are safe. From a young age, we create images of ourselves, pretending to be what we think other people want us to be. Then we project these images onto our relationships and try our best to be the images. But of course, we can't ever conform to someone else's vision. And this is how inner conflict originates. When people start to feel a discrepancy between the image they're projecting, and their authentic selves, major conflict arises within them.

> "And the day came when the risk to remain tight in a bud was more painful than the risk it took to blossom."
>
> **Anais Nin**

Believe more deeply, enter a world of unlimited possibilities, and imagine what amazing opportunities are there waiting for you as you walk along that path, or through that new door that is wide open. Once you start acknowledging what you know to be true to you which is the reason you are reading this book, you will be ready, the vision is already taking shape.

Rome wasn't built in a night. Say I am ready to walk through that door knowing there is something more out there for me to live a life fulfilled with joy and happiness. It is accepting the fear of doubt, what we have already built up inside of us which remember this has made you the person you are today.

Believe that right now you are perfectly perfect. You can have the life you may have considered a privilege, a life that only designed for the rich and famous. Do you know how I know this? because I am living proof.

> *"Listen to your heart – and honour it."*
>
> **Emily Gowor**

As a young child, I believe we have superpowers

Chapter 4
Be Yourself

"The real difficulty is to overcome how you think about yourself. If we don't have that we never grow, we never learn, and sure as hell we should never teach."

Maya Angelou

The only person holding you back is YOU

Being yourself means living life how you want to live, regardless of other people's opinions. It means you respect yourself. Not worrying about what others think. You can't control them or their thoughts. Interestingly they are thinking the same way you are.

As a young child, I believe we have superpowers. I would act out different characters, nothing could stand in my way until mealtimes when expected to be home, I would daydream about what I wanted to be when I grew up.

As I reached puberty there was a knowing I wanted to make something of myself, but something was holding me back.

I would spend more time and energy in wanting to fit in and want people to like me. I experienced bullying at school, I gave up my power to others and allowed myself worth to be knocked over, and over again.

The response by my mother to my problems in school when I would return home upset would be, they are bitches, fight back or don't hang out with them and find some new friends.

After many years, even into my early adulthood, I kept doing the same thing. I had the power at any time to stop this vicious cycle, but I didn't know how to activate it. I felt powerless.

Back in the day, and still today even tall poppy syndrome is rife. No one would want to stand out, and if they did you were shot down in flames. It is hard to imagine that anyone could have that type of control over you, again feeling of powerlessness.

The key for me was to get my life back, take back the control I always had, however, was afraid to exercise 'Tall Poppy'. I was still afraid of what people would think about me. Quite interestingly I was tall in my day and would try to shrink myself, and had a head full of red hair, and tried my hardest not to stand out.

We live in a culture that is starving for authenticity. We want our leaders, co-workers, family members, friends, and anyone we interact with tell us the truth and be themselves.

Most importantly, we want the personal freedom and confidence to make our own decision based on our own thoughts and feelings without worrying about how we appear to others, and what they may think or say about us.

Even though we may say we want to live in truth, aligned with our beliefs and identify with them, and our desires, most of us don't. We have been taught by our parents, teachers, spouses, friends, co-workers, politicians, the media, and others, that it's more important to be liked and to fit in than it is to be who we truly are.

In addition, many of us assume that who we are is not good enough and therefore we're constantly trying to fix ourselves or to act like others who we think are better than us.

Although we may have learnt similar things, we produce a different kind of results with our knowledge and skills we are blessed with.

Reminds me of the quote Albert Einstein was widely accredited for "The definition of insanity is doing the same thing over and over again but expecting different results."

Being ourselves is about enjoying a new sense of freedom to be who we really are naturally in all aspects of our lives without a mask.

It takes much courage, commitment, and depth to look within ourselves, to tell the whole truth, to be vulnerable and to admit, own and share our real thoughts, feelings, desires, insecurities, passions, blunders, dreams and more.

Let's face it, most of us get in our own way. We indulge in self-doubt, self-sabotage, and mind games like "I don't deserve this," or "I'm not good enough."

Being in the flow is a conscious choice

Change is imminent and something quite often we can resist as sometimes we feel pain through the change. However, the more we can change and adapt the easier you can move through the pain of change.

We are not meant to stay static, and movement is required as in exercise walking, cycling whatever floats your boat. Listening to your body and know what it needs allows us to be in that flow much better.

I have been practising this for some time now and there are still times I ignore my thoughts and feelings, and the result is out of the flow, feeling low or heavy body just feeling like crap basically. I know it feels hard, impossible even sometimes or a lot of the time, but you can make it through this.

Listen to your inner self, the spiritual you, conscious you are saying, you are stronger than anyone I have ever known. I am always by your side, bringing you strength in your time of need. Together we can do anything.

I started writing on different topics relevant, to help people, to help myself, as I knew with every fibre, I wanted to be able to make a positive impact in the world.

I loved writing inspirational words have been doing that for a decade. It led to writing blogs around autism as that was my experience at the time. To help people navigate their way through life to support their struggles, to create some ease rather DIS-ease.

By doing this, the process helped me and in turn, I could help others. If my cup was half empty rather than half full, then I could never offer you a drink from my cup.

Key principles for being your self

A way to utilise your individual power in your life to enhance your relationships, increase your fulfilment, and empower yourself, here are some key principles:

Know Yourself – Commit to your own personal growth. Discover more of who you are. And, seek out and allow the support, honest feedback, and guidance of others.

Transform Your Fear – There's nothing wrong with being afraid it's the resistance and denial of fear that can be the real problem. Acting in the face of fear is courageous and empowering.

Express Yourself – Dare to speak your truth and deal with conflicts directly. Be vulnerable and real about what you think and how you feel and be able to express your emotions fully. While on the surface you may think this will be seen as "weak," in fact expressing yourself completely gives you access to real freedom and power. I cry all the time! Embrace and celebrate the tears and don't question them as you go through this process allow them to surface.

Be Bold – Live, speak, and act with courage, passion, and truth no matter how overwhelming it may seem. Go for what you want in your work and in life. Get back up when you seem like you are falling. We've got this.

Celebrate You – Appreciate and honour you, what you do, and the gifts and talents you bring. It is not about arrogance if coming from the heart. It's an amazing awareness of your own power, and it's the key to self-confidence, joy and fulfilment.

Always choose yourself first

When are you able to say "no" and when are you considered unkind and without compassion, simply unwilling?

Especially, for the ones that are very conscious about themselves, it is very difficult to draw boundaries. We understand people as a result of our own (previous) suffering. We do not want other people to go through the same as they end up being used as doormats.

This is NOT what we want. We want to stand in our own power be the person we signed up to when we entered the physical realm. We want to show people that we are kind and loving beings, but also that we certainly have our limits.

There are many people jumping for your help. They see how your eyes light up and they want what you have. You are the trusted adviser and you know how to provide the key to help others. However, you can't help others if you are not feeling well yourself. You will be giving away what you do not have yet.

First, loving yourself, healing yourself and feeling good about yourself, then you can take the step to serve or help others effectively and when you are in a good place.

When you feel low in energy, become aware of when this happens, and withdraw from people that just look out for your help or attention, because it won't provide you with any lasting energy. It needs to be a win/win situation.

Stay in our own truth, our own business is the key. The many people on this planet all have their own differing opinions, experiences and visions which is none of our business, unless they ask for your opinion don't give it.

The hardest lesson I found was staying out of others business, but once you nail it everyone can go about living their own business.

Does that mean anyone is wrong? No, that is the thing, there is no right or wrong. There is only right and wrong for you. This is the picture you draw for yourself. Which of the opinions I want to take in, and I resonate with? And which of the opinions do not fit my reality.

You are here to learn and find out what is true for you. Where do your interests lie? What makes you smile and ignites that something in you? If you stick to what you love to do, you can be sure there is no one else going up against it.

Think about it, we look up to the people who have found their passion and true purpose. "They are so sure of themselves", I wish I was like that... You can be! Just stick to what you love and live to what inspires you.

I hope that provided you with some clarity. It is with open-heartedness I see every day in my HR role, many people are looking for something more, a change, and generally look outside of themselves rather than inside where all the action happens, however then dealing with the pain may seem too much to bare.

As a recommendation stay true to yourself, do what you love and follow your own internal guidance system, which I refer to as your internal GPS.

Being your true self is not for the faint-hearted, but once you're willing to truly engage and do the work, your life, your work, and your relationships will be more exciting, meaningful, and fulfilling.

We were all born with our own individual talents, there is no way we can compare ourselves to other people. We can learn from each other, but we are all unique in our own way.

Cycles of life

The cycles of Life - People come and go and understanding that everyone who enters our sphere appears for a reason, not by coincidence, but by design. They are like mirrors of ourselves, this might be a mirror that we like, or that we do not like.

We generally avoid the mirror we do not like as that creates pain and feeling of discomfort. We need to work on what we do not like so that we can create a life that we can prosper.

Uncomfortable is the new comfortable - You are not in your power when you are in the same state for extended periods. Sadness is normal and should be embraced for what it is.

After the period of sadness, there is a recovery period in which you set the pace to be open for new things in life again. It's like yin (female energy) and yang (masculine energy), darkness and lightness. happiness and sadness. We can't have one without the other. The difference is how long we stay in any one state.

Each cycle is wonderful on their own, or as you may see it right now, as not feeling yourself or feeling crap. It is not about forgetting it is about creating new space for new experiences to arrive.

I emphasise that life is a journey, and it is dependent upon how long we hold on to something that doesn't feel right. Self-acceptance plays a big part, rather than criticising yourself, accept that piece of you, that feeling which brought you to where you are today to your perfect state of being, how can you regret perfection. You may not be able to see it, but I can. Start seeing it and feeling into it. Who says we are not perfect?

Quote daily to self, "I love and accept you, you are perfect in every way, Thank you."

Stop comparing yourself to others

When you compare yourself to others constantly, you will always feel inferior, that you are lacking in something. There will always be someone who appears to have more than you, who is better than you. We create this story from learned behaviours, and experiences being shown through the media that show only the positive and successful people.

Seems that is how we want to see the world and others. We are all on the same journey, we just bring different skills, and each of us is unique in what we do, and how we serve others, as ultimately that is what we are here to do, and create a life to thrive in during the process.

Have you ever considered that everything we see from outside of us is an illusion? What is insignificant to others, could be everything for you.

What can I do to feel those things that I want to achieve in my life? What do I need to change to obtain what I would really love to achieve? Start with questions and watch the magic, get very clear, and then create your own life path. Yes, you CAN do it. I believe in you.

Avoid negative energy - Not reasonable to expect we can be happy and entertaining all day. If a job you do requires this would make sense that downtime would be quieter time if you are living in your truth so not expecting this from yourself.

We can choose the people we would like to hang with, our own tribe the relatable people and guess what they don't have to be your existing family. You can choose your family, you have permission. Just reflecting on comparing yourself to others is when you draw the people that may not fit congruently and may just be causing you the pain.

People with low energy and always negative, get caught up in the drama and other business, will suck the life out of you. Once you are on the journey to awareness and creating a more fulfilling life you will just keep wanting more and could come in the form of a change in job, friend circles as you grow as a person. We all need to grow by nourishing our minds and bodies.

Conclusion of inner power - Something we all have. The saying, happiness is an inside job is true. We look for happiness outside of us to others or things.

Inner power is the inner knowing that all will be okay again. It is the intuition, the knowledge that what you want to achieve will happen. It is the person that recognises that everything you put into action, the kindness you show, you will receive back tenfold.

Sitting at home without any action won't bring you what you want. Find something you like doing and do that thing. Money, recognition, inspirations and like-minded people only cross your path when you are in alignment with what you want to achieve in life.

Daily habits to reclaim your life

Habit stacking is my new term. This means to create a new, good habit in your daily routine, get good at it, and then create another one, keep stacking.

I never create New Year's resolutions; I create new habits and stack them. They can be something as simple as rearranging your cutlery draw.

I rearranged the cutlery draw one day, and I thought about what I noticed after the change as this is the important part of the natural process, is to notice. I felt more organised, less cluttered, and felt some order in my life. Everything you do or change is a reflection of your life.

How are those daily habits coming along from previous chapters? Keep yourself accountable, or better still find an accountability partner. It's easy to slip back into the old ways.

One of my daily main purpose statements I can share to recovering myself – "During this time, I learnt many new observations about myself and others. I will now use my newfound knowledge by implementing it in my work, life, family and MYSELF."

Goal setting - Setting goals, having a vision (bigger the better), hairy bodacious goals are very important aspects to one's life. Without any goals, your life seems meaningless and your inner power stays dormant. Go out there and explore what life has to offer you.

Listen with the intent to your intuition, your inner knowing and keep journaling that was my secret to connect with myself, it started with a scribble, anger, resentment, stuff that I felt I could never say out loud, or talk to anyone about, however on paper knowing that this was for my ears and eyes only I could say and express to my heart's content.

Listen with the intent to others – Most people do not listen with the intent to understand, most listen with the intent to reply. Our ability to listen is an essential skill for those responsible for leading and managing people at every level. Be interested, not interesting.

Let us aspire to be the leader in world change. The current system isn't working so well and so it's up to us now. It always was really we have just woken from a long sleep.

We live and do work with a driving passion to improve the wellbeing of our world.

I wanted to share and encourage all women on this journey to 'discover and recover their true identity'

Chapter 5
Lost Identity

"People often say that this or that person has not yet found himself. But the self is not something one finds; it is something one creates."

Thomas Szasz

Feeling alone and helpless

Don't go, don't leave me? These are words I said to myself when I knew change was imminent. I was a frightened little girl who knew what was behind me was scarier than what was ahead of me but where to start.

I was lost never to be found and caught in the search for the meaning of life. The crisis in itself is in epidemic proportion, which is no surprise, and knowing you are not alone.

It is a great personal tragedy to wakeup not caring anymore, not wanting to try anymore, it is almost like there is this tearful desperation in your heart because your heart knows more, your heart knows better. I believe 98% of the world just want to be heard. It's that simple.

Knowing something was missing, the tools for the rough terrain that I was experiencing. I wasn't equipped, I didn't have the solid foundations, but I was a survivor and I knew one thing was for sure I needed to be resilient somehow. It was a process, and each step I needed to be open to accept help, be the change, and allow myself to be vulnerable.

My fears kicked in and I was afraid of what my life might look like if I was to change. It had happened before, and relationships ended. Would my family still be in the picture? Just reminded me of the movie 'Back to the Future when everyone was starting to fade out of the photo, as the future was changing.

I knew at that moment I had to let go of that idea, as it would not serve anyone, in particular myself to stay somewhere when it was time to move on to the next stage of my life. I knew deep within my heart to find out who I truly am, the soul sister was definitely going to experience some discomfort to unravel that needed to be revealed.

If someone had asked me ten years ago who 'Karen Howe' is, I would have said I don't know other than a fun party girl, a wife and a mum. If that was to be my legacy shoot me now.

I recall asking myself is my only role in life to be a mother and wife? I just seemed to have 'lost the joy' in my roles. At that moment I was experiencing the awakening, I knew I wanted to share and encourage all wives and mothers on this journey to 'recovering your identity'.

Always attracting the same people wherever I travelled, there was no escape really no matter where I went it was just the places that changed, not the people. I needed to break the cycle of people I invited into my life, those that were in alignment with me however that was only going to happen with being true to who I am.

"Let them go. Your destiny is never tied to anyone who leaves you. And it doesn't mean they're bad people. It just means that their part of the story is over."

Julia Roberts

Whilst writing this chapter the story in my head is like the chorus to a song. I lost my identity. It's not lost it just got buried amongst the rubble, the noise, the people that say you can't do that, or say this, or that, or be this, or that, or have this or that.

The journey to self-discovery

The journey of self-discovery should be an important goal for everyone. Some people go through life playing a role to mask who they really are. Others simply become what others want them to be. "Know thyself" is a classic sentiment that continues to offer a valuable reminder today.

It is only through the discovery of self that we can identify our purpose and build on our potential. On the other hand, failure to embark on a journey of self-discovery will cheat us of the opportunity to understand who we are and what we want out of life, as well as how we can help others during our time on this earth.

So highly recommend until you have some control of your life, to improve your negative state, turn off the world noise, or learn to be selective to allow your mind to be open to new and exciting opportunities.

Have you noticed there is so much sadness and anger in the world which you can do absolutely nothing about, so why put yourself through the agony of what is happening in the world?

I am not suggesting close your feelings off, but just watch the magic when you remove the drama, the distractions that have absolutely nothing to do with you. Everything outside of ourselves is absolutely none of our business.

People say to me how do you do all that you do? There is a quote that if you want a job done give it to a busy person. I enjoy my life and what I do now which gives me more time back as I am not wasting it sitting in space that doesn't serve me in how I might feel about something, or someone, and stewing over something that has nothing to do with me, and resolves in time I can't get back.

This is not negotiable if you want to lead a happy fulfilled life which if you are reading this suggests you do. Yes, it requires changes in your current existence, and adapting but can I tell you, it's worth it.

If you feel judgement by anyone which you will (yes tall poppy syndrome alert) just know they will come back into your life if they are meant to be there, as they will want what you have now. If they don't then it was time for them to move on, as you did. We can't hold anyone back that needs to leave and grow differently, you are now needing new teachers in your life.

Learning life skills is what change is all about. We can't expect to stay the same even though we have tried to do that we know that we need to grow. We can't hold ourselves back because of others opinions of us.

I would have people that don't understand or support what I do and that is perfectly okay, however, we still love each other. It should not matter what you do in life what matters is that you create your own life, and everything will fall into place around that. You will be in the flow, gorgeous being.

As I speak with people and discuss how I came to do what I do and all the things in my life to increase my level of confidence, and showing up in the world to make a difference everyone says confidence is the last thing you are lacking Karen.

Here's the trick: even the most confident have the doubting days when they second guess or go into a downward spiral about the next project or meeting etc. This is because we have to push ourselves which requires a daily routine including daily personal development, mantras, whatever that new habit is to embrace change and allows less mind chatter and more action.

You owe it to yourself to work on yourself daily.

To find out who you are and what you are meant to be doing rather than reliving the same story.

It occurred to me I spent my life 'creating' an identity, so much energy poured into that when I already had my own blueprint, the original magnificent masterpiece which I had learnt not to trust.

It was like accessorising. Excuse me, god, could I upgrade please to that person over there, I like how that person thinks, and speaks, and the confidence is exactly what I want, so I will add that to my order as well.

I look back and giggle to myself which I can do now and say how could I have been so lost. Looking in the mirror and talking to yourself is where it starts. Be kind and offer words of hope as if you were offering to a child.

Generally, anything that draws attention to us we avoid, as it forces us to experience the pain and hurt but ignoring allows it to keep showing up at some point impacting our health and wellbeing.

When I reached this awakening state, I was prepared to do almost anything to feel again and be on my journey to helping others discover and recover their identity.

Vulnerability and connection

Writing this book was one of the toughest gigs, sharing my vulnerability with the world to get the message out there.

Whilst writing this book I travelled overseas to spend time with my older son. I flew out from Australia to London, Athens, Santorini, Paris, London and home again. Felt blessed that I had this opportunity to travel by myself with myself for myself.

As a solo traveller, I was constantly practising vulnerability. Vulnerability is a powerful thing, and the practice underrated. It is something that opens us up to a world of connection and community. But it also exposes us to the possibility of pain and heartbreak. You need to find the courage to open yourself up all the while knowing that there is a fairly good chance that one day you will be hurt.

Why should I care about opening myself up to people you may be asking?

In the example of travel, it is all about connection and to form connections you need to be vulnerable.

As human beings, we tend to avoid pain. It's only natural. No one wants to get their heart broken or experience emotional pain. We avoid situations that are likely to get us into trouble because it stems from an instinct to protect ourselves. But when we put walls up to protect ourselves from pain which results in distancing ourselves from love and connection.

We have lost the subtle art of connection we lost this aspect to us which is the only true thing that we are. It's all we are, is how we connect and how we communicate with others. It is the only currency, in how we leave others feeling when they leave our presence.

My work is not to tell others how to live their lives as that is already happening in society, however, I endeavor to offer a different perspective to get your mind thinking about something from a different angle so that you can connect with your own truth. I don't want your truth to be my truth either, it needs to be aligned with your truth. You're the hero in your story that's what this is all about.

The process is really straight forward we need to turn what seems like a problem into an opportunity. We want people like yourself who are already looking for more, to get excited about life again. Life as you knew it as a child. Remember what that was like.

Manifesting a life void of meaning doesn't have to be that way. I hope that from some of my struggles you realise that you are not alone in life with your own struggles. I would hope that once you go from fear to a limitless life will inspire you to write a book, share your experiences with others. It's closing the gap on limiting lives to enhancing.

It's one hundred percent what you are telling yourself so be careful about what you are saying. It is just a thought.

You have to master your mind by mastering your thoughts and manage your emotions. I took up personal development fulltime, it became my qualification. I decided my new qualification and the area I would spend time on was personal development, life skills which I would never learn in any institution.

What you are today is a reflection of your thoughts and your mind. To become someone different you have to do different actions. The second you decide to do things differently, you go into the river of change, transformation, your body gets uncomfortable, you hear voices saying you are not worthy enough, you can't handle it because being comfortable you have to fight those thoughts.

It takes consistent daily action to make changes, but you've got this, or you wouldn't have got this far as to pick up this book.

Once I decided it was massive action however, I noticed things improve very quickly at the flick of a change of thought switch. Every single person on this planet matters. You matter your story matters.

If you help one person you have made a difference. You get to decide what is it you want, what is it you are going to create. You feel it in your heart in your entire being. Every single day you will be in action. If you believe in self, you will be unstoppable.

When I was young and free my imagination had no limits, I dreamed of changing the world.

Daily habits to reclaim your life

Remove the bad news from your life – listen to the highlights if you need to hear about what's going on in the news. My mother laughs at me and says how will you know if you need to evacuate? I said you will call me and tell me before the relevant services do.

Research every day, read, listen to an audio something to inspire you. Do something for yourself that you enjoy. You are allowed, to do something for you and the more you do it just gets better.

Write down a list of things you want. Sit with it and say it out loud whilst maintaining your posture so you need to write the things you believe to be true for you.

Be grateful for something every day and grow that bodacious gratitude list. Write the things you are grateful for and revisit these regularly.

Consistency is important even if you multitask.

You can be listening to your audio in the car travelling or whilst exercising. The key is what are you listening to that will create joy in your life.

Do something for self every day to support you, something you like something special, because you are worth it

Remove friends from your life that no longer support you

Create and continue to refine / review your vision, mission & values. Place them somewhere you can see and live by them. This is your why, and who you are.

My vision and mission are kept simple in summary, to serve and equip people with the tools to thrive, and as a natural consequence will inspire and transform the lives of many.

Values I stand for: Inspiration, Greatness, Fulfilment, Spirituality, Self-expression, Wisdom, Love, Hope

Qualities of my brand include: Female, Power (the ability to act effectively), & Inspiration

Smile or hug a stranger every day and say thank you.

Learn to compliment people around you.

"You are looking incredible, that colour really does work for you."

"Thank you for your gift of kindness"

Try to avoid saying things like "You didn't have to do that." or what I hear a lot of and I did this myself, was to apologise all the time, like your apologising you were born. Be kind to yourself and stop apologising.

If you feel you have offended someone you can reply with "I didn't mean to offend you." Don't apologise for anything as you would not say or do anything to harm anyone intentionally would you? No, we all care about each other, we just need to mind our language, and change it where we feel we need to.

I created a wall around myself bigger than the Great Wall of China

Chapter 6

Wearing A Mask For The World

"I was tired of pretending that I was someone else just to get along with people, just for the sake of having friendships."

Kurt Cobain

Don't wait to be accepted

Don't wait to be accepted, accept yourself. I was a high functioning zombie crippled with fear to love, fear to trust, fear of abandonment again. I was always someone who craved love and attention.

I wanted to be anyone except myself, in fact, I worked hard to become someone else. I was living the imposter syndrome outwardly. We can easily put on the mask for the world, however, the outside needs to match the inside.

People would say to me I don't understand you are so confident and know your stuff, however inwardly I was terrified and did an excellent job at covering that inward feeling.

Being on my path to self-discovery I am now forced to see these elements that no longer serve me and make the necessary changes.

Just like when you go into a new role at work you need to learn new skills to do the job well. It's about creating new skills/habits in your life. Change and adapt is as important as breathing. I know I talk about change a lot but that is how we move forward however being able to adapt is the key. Ready, set, go 'Change'.

Until then even though I felt an impostor and wasn't able to distinguish right from wrong or the truth, I was living in a fantasy world and wanted to stay that little girl forever waiting for my daddy to say 'I love you' I would wait and wait.

It didn't work once I got to 18 years of age bigger expectations were upon me. I am now 57 so the thoughts I had as an 18-year-old are not going to work for me anymore, just leaving me feeling empty.

I still hadn't learnt to leave people who incinerated me which would release me from the imprisonment of self-sabotage. I had set myself up, and without knowing was walking into more unhappiness.

I had a clear description of what I didn't want to be, but growing up in a family where you were not supported as everyone was in survival mode right? They didn't have the tools themselves.

I wasn't of the age to even consider leaving home I was terrified. I thought I know if I just create a life being the best version of Karen, as talked about in the previous chapter I would look around the room and seek attributes in others I thought would serve me. This charade went on for many years to come.

Wearing the mask

Wearing a mask or facade for me was "Fake it till you make it" an English aphorism which suggests that by imitating confidence, competence, and an optimistic mindset, a person can realise those qualities in their real life.

We all have three faces. The first face you show to the world. The second face you show to your family and close friends. The third face you never show anyone. It is the truest reflection of who you are.

Showing your true face is something you are simply incapable of doing. It's a face that you probably only trust your significant other with seeing. Obviously, you have the first face because you need to have a sort of standing in society. You must have a certain level of professionalism at work and etiquette in society.

The second face is more relaxed. You're able to be more "you". You don't have to put up a wall, or at least as much of a wall, in front of the people you trust.

However, that third face? That is you, even the bits that scare you. Even the bits that you don't like to acknowledge or even recognise as you. Even the corny bits and the bits that think both terrible and beautiful things that you'd never normally share with others. That part of you which is sacred.

It echoes the underlying principles of cognitive behavioural therapy to enable a change in one's behaviour. I just kept following the rinse and repeat method seemed to work or so I thought until the day I felt so disconnected the cracks in my mask were starting to show.

I didn't feel the need for love and now began creating a wall to protect myself. A wall that was bigger than the great wall of china.

Growing up in a society that constantly tells us what to say, how to think, how we should feel, what to be when we grow up, and then how to act in public is unrealistic as we are all very unique, affording us varying perspectives.

It would not be fair for me to pass on my advice, because everyone's life is different and so is their journey. Writing this book if I didn't write from my perspective, and had asked everyone's opinion, I would not have given the book justice as I needed to come from my heart and my truth. I provide experiences in this book, and if it makes a difference and resonates with others who read it, then I have achieved much.

When my husband who is a singer songwriter and co-producer was asked what inspired him to write a song. His response was just the emotion and the storytelling.

We want to inspire others, so we show them they are not alone and that the most well-accomplished individuals around you still need to work on it and take the necessary action. This book like songs will draw on and connect with your emotion from an experience in your life. I hope that makes sense.

The victim of circumstance

Remember it took me until early 50's to know there was more, and to figure out what that meant, and if I wanted to live my life knowing what was important to me, and where my time was spent, to allow me to make a difference in the world I needed to be that change.

Until then I must wear the mask.

I needed to be clear on what my message was and how I was going to deliver that message. Every day is a new opportunity to make a change in our lives we are no longer coming from a child's mind we are now all grown up honouring the child or the person that paved the way for you.

We all know change is uncomfortable however it will be more uncomfortable to stay where we are. I was born perfect until the age of seven, but something happened after that magical age. We become more aware and now in my experience with my own children, it's about them knowing they are safe and ensuring we play a part in their lives, enjoy being involved in what they love, being interested, not being interesting.

I never felt safe, in fact, I lived in terror as a child, I never knew when dad was going to get drunk and be abusive. I never knew when my mother would leave us so always left me wondering if she would be there when I got home from school.

I couldn't even leave home as I was this wounded little girl with no one to talk. You didn't talk about what happened at home you just didn't period.

Every day we are in conflict, feel the victim of circumstances. Were fascinated with body language If we can understand what that feeling is that keeps us stuck and living Groundhog Day then we can continue to move toward that thing that makes us smile and want to live every day as if we were in Disneyland. To reach for the stars!

Sometimes, however, for us to notice the feelings can be painful, can bring up a lot of stuff that we have avoided for so long. We have held it close to our hearts for too long. The stuff that creates DIS-ease in our bodies. The stuff that is generally not ours as it's a learned behaviour generated from experience or something we have witnessed as a child and held on to that experience.

Then you can be guaranteed that we will act out that behaviour at the most inappropriate time and childlike response.

For those of you that wonder why most people hide their true face from the world? Ask yourself the same question, because even you do it, even if unconscious.

> *"You never really understand a person until you consider things from his point of view until you climb into his skin and walk around in it."*
>
> **Atticus, To Kill a Mockingbird**

We need to understand the dynamics of the game as it is not difficult just complex.

An example using Porky pig who was the victim of a cartoon character I grew up with...Bugs bunny handles the attack and deals with it, really doesn't let the situation affect him too much. He Laughs about it. We tend to get involved in the story i.e. Elma Fudd blaming bugs bunny.

My parents would always say never walk into a room sulking, so I would stay confined to my bedroom as this is how I am feeling today. You cannot hide your true feelings however this is what we learn to do when it is brought to our attention.

We have those learned behaviours that once we upgrade our inner system, we get to experience the most amazing things, some small, some on a larger scale, however, love everything that comes into your life for the good of mankind.

If you feel sad or not feeling the love, be kind to yourself and know that feeling is okay. Know that this too shall pass, and you will be rocking that feeling again.

Who makes the rules up any way of what we should be, do or say! YOU, not your parents, not the authorities, not your circle of friends. Not putting a face on for the world is being your authentic self.

In the words of Oscar Wild, "Be yourself; everyone else is already taken."

Journal your feelings and fears

I didn't want to cause myself any more harm; I wanted to connect and understand how I operated instead.

Writing things down served as a great way of releasing that which no longer serves me where I am at in my life right now. I am not that nine-year-old anymore.

Grab that journal with the exclusive intention of putting your emotions into words. Try and pinpoint when and what makes you feel good or sad.

By putting everything on paper you can then reference your emotions, investigate your behavioural patterns, and recognise what made you feel a certain way and how you dealt with it. I never beat myself up once recognised I now go through the self-acceptance process. "That experience got me to where I am today, how beautiful is that, because I am perfect."

Keeping a journal ensures connection to self so you can make real changes that last forever. Be ready for that amazing change knowing that is a time to grow.

Risk trusting other people

Instead of testing people in my life, I let go and grant people access. I decided that even if someone let me down, I could deal with it.

Moving circles helped. I got back in touch with people I liked growing up, and I was surprised to find that many were happy to reconnect with me.

This was not easy however I didn't make it about me, I got out of my own way and put myself on the line and trusted my instincts to contact these people. As I started to feel more connected and less alone, I realised this move paid off.

I decided to be open with new people that came into my life. I didn't scare them off at the first encounter, but as relationships began to develop, I would explain how my past affected me, and how I'd chosen to move on and be happy.

Almost everyone I was open to was completely supportive. Openness became a two-way street. I learned that most people had experienced their own struggles. Our confessions strengthened these new relationships.

I also learned that not everyone is someone I can be open to—but the more I do it, the better instincts I have about who to let into my life. Taking risks with people is essential for happiness.

Let go of or better still be accepting of old stories

I have let go of the negative feelings around my mother. I realised that I was heading up a similar path to her, and this taught me to feel compassion for her.

I have released all the negativity I held toward her, and now I just hope that one day she can learn to love herself.

I have forgiven my ex-husband and even thanked him for the lesson I learnt about managing my own finances. I now just hope he can forgive himself.

In order to let go, I needed to understand my mother. I had painted my own picture and I told myself this is not fair to her. Her life has come about through her own experiences during her childhood, and it is not any of my business to judge her.

By looking at her in this way, I could see that her abandoning us had nothing to do with me. If she hadn't had me and had given birth to another daughter, it would have been the same outcome.

Once I realised that our unhealthy non-relationship wasn't my fault, I was able to stop blaming her and hanging onto the victim story.

Once you stop telling the story, it has less power over you.

Love yourself

In the past, I tried to hide from myself, and all this did was make me lose myself further. By braving up and removing the escape methods, I have found my raw being.

Vulnerability is not a negative state. It is how we start on our path.

By loving myself, I allow others to love me. I love myself because I am still here, and I can see my life changing around me. When I have moments of insecurity, I read through my journals, speak to friends, or throw myself into tasks I enjoy, like writing, staying connected, and walking.

Since changing my outlook, I have started my own business, with daily journaling, writing this book, running workshops, and supporting others with their transformation. Listening to what is relevant to all aspects of their lives and where their concerns are.

Those areas in our lives things that are stopping them or holding them back from so many opportunities and unlimited possibilities that present themselves all the time which we either ignore, that no doubt may never have even a consideration because of the stories we are telling ourselves that we are not enough. I am here to tell you that you are enough.

I went from the wounded child (victim) to living a life that I wake up every day feeling energised and want to make a difference in the world positively. I feel now I can help others do the same.

I have trained myself to work on a positive mindset to come from helping someone positively, is more powerful than coming from a victim mentality. It takes daily training and I now know there is no turning back.

The important thing is to allow ourselves to open to other loving relationships. At my age I want to feel, taste, touch, experience everything and anything possible without making sacrifices just being myself.

I decided to say YES to most things because I know the positive change that comes from saying YES as to the feeling you're left with when saying NO because of your circumstances where you replace your dreams with you don't have time or money. This is when we make sacrifices that are not congruent to who we are

Who says challenges are a bad thing or fear is negative? Perception plays a key role in holding us up because of the energy behind these words and what they mean to us from our experience when we heard someone talk or act out something which we then labelled.

I have learnt there is no right or wrong just a series of deductions either fear-based or fearless. What story or beliefs are you running with? Are you making some bold decisions and evolving? All that you have ever dreamed of you already are. Just permit yourself.

Daily habits to reclaim your life

Take some time to uncover all three faces.

You may find it easier to write about one or two faces. Take the time though, to explore all three.

You will find that each face informs the other two, and as you reveal each one, you will add dimension to your character and help you connect even more deeply.

Which face have you focused on most? Which face do you find most challenging to write?

You can create your life, or
you can allow others
to create it for you

Chapter 7
Surviving to Thriving

"The only thing that holds you back from getting what you want is paying attention to what you don't want."
"The achievement of anything that you desire must be considered success, whether it is a trophy or money or relationships or things. ... You've got a desire.

Abraham Hicks

There was an important time in my life I was abandoned, my mother left us for another man, and whilst knowing what I know now she was seeking refuge from an unhappy marriage.

I am blessed that I got to understand this was not about me, but her happiness, and she needed to put herself first as she deserved a better life. As a nine-year-old, you don't see this.

She returned and continued to live in an unhappy relationship, the only one she knew.

People generally stay in unhappy situations because they are comfortable and too scared of what is on the other side.

You cannot be one of those people, because you deserve to live the life you desire.

I now believe people are put in our path to show us the way. You can make it about them, or you can make it about yourself. You can create your life, or you can allow them to create it for you. Which do you want?

Life happens for you, not to you

We all struggle with insecurities, and because of these insecurities, we try to justify situations that aren't right for us - whether it's a job, money, relationships or a friendship. I myself have and still can struggle with the insecurities brought on by my past. It's more than just physical insecurities, but the idea that sometimes I feel like I'm too damaged or like I've been through too much in my life.

I was born into a family that was in survival mode. That was my lot and I couldn't run or change from my situation as I was too young. There was no one to say here are some tools to help you as we were all in the same boat paddling upstream without the paddle. It came naturally to be a survivor as all I had ever known.

My thinking was maybe I'm just too screwed up, and thus incapable of being loved because of the struggles of my past.

Sometimes I wish my parents had not stayed together when I was nine maybe then I would have had an attentive, complete mother to raise me, and maybe life would have been different.

Maybe if I had not been treated like complete crap in my past relationships, I would not be so scared to give all of myself to someone again.

Maybe if my father hadn't passed away in his prime years, I'd be less scarred, and I wouldn't get sad seeing a father and daughter laughing and sharing their lives, or when a father spending time with grandkids and watch them grow, and attend their special and meaningful occasions.

All of the stories running in my head did not get me anywhere but curled up in my bed crying about things I cannot change. I've realised you have to learn to manage these feelings, not dismiss them, but acknowledge knowing everything that happens in life that may either seem good, or bad, are things that got you to where you are today.

Are these thoughts still serving me?

It's the now that we ask the questions moving forward, do these thoughts, things and feelings still serve me? It's about recognising when change is required, then moving from surviving to thriving which is your entitlement.

Those thoughts, things and feelings that don't make you smile, that don't add value, and people who don't make you feel the way you should, happy, loved and beautiful, then you're ready for this change.

There is nothing to say you are stuck with those that are incapable of loving you. Nothing is predicting your life will be spent lonely or unfulfilled. You are the one that can say, I have got this.

Courage to change

It takes courage to change the way you think, your beliefs, learned behaviours, however to move forward to create an amazing life for yourself where you feel enriched and naturally happy you have to close the old wounds you've been left with from whatever relationship, traumatic experience or getting fired from a job you loved/hated you have to close these wounds for yourself, and by yourself.

On those nights when you feel alone, like no one will understand you or have the answers to your questions, remember that aloneness is designed to help you discover who you are so that you'll stop looking outside yourself for your worth. You already have everything you need to be complete right here, right now in this very moment.

So, when that boyfriend, husband, wife, sister, brother, friend constantly takes advantage of you and puts you down you will eventually build the strength to take nothing less than what you deserve.

When you're working day in, and day out at a company that doesn't value your opinion, your knowledge, or your boss is a complete arse for no apparent reason other than the fact that he/she is unhappy with his/her own miserable life you'll have the confidence to seek out a new career and find a company that appreciates and values you as a person.

I was only nine years of age and already felt my life was spiralling out of control. I was this lost and confused little girl born into a family that the only way they knew how to live was to just survive.

To show what is possible

It was no fault of their own that was all they knew. In fact, I have even spent time saying thank you and sending love to each one of my family and people that have shown up in my life to show me what is possible.

I took over the reins, and said I got this, and was the conductor of my own orchestra.

My mother has been declining in her health since she was 65, now in aged care in a wheel chair I knew that if I didn't change my way of thinking and create a life to thrive and draw those people into my life, then that could be me.

When I recently asked my mother what her biggest regret was, her response was marrying my father. When you ask a question, be ready for the answer even if you don't like it.

What it did show was the lack of love and care, remember however she was still in survival mode, had not learned her own lessons, and I knew within my heart I couldn't save her now as a child that's what you want to do save your parents.

I am no longer a child, I am a 57-year-old woman.

You will find someone who will love you through success and failure so that you can discover how little life has to do with either.

I had felt broken until one day talking to my trusted advisor (friend), that held no judgement, said I do not think you are broken. Your background and the family you were born into are survivors, and that was all you knew, was how to survive.

The way I see it you are a person who knows the difference between what is right and what is wrong. Try to remember that your relationship with your family also helped to shape those parts. They helped you become who you are today.

Her brokenness bestowed upon her such compassion and grace and a gratitude for every one of her challenges and difficult experiences as they opened her heart wider and blessed her with unconditional love.

So, when you feel unlucky, or you start to feel bad about yourself take a second to see how far you have come. You may have been criticising yourself for years which no longer works for you.

Try accepting yourself and everything that has happened in your life as being beautiful and watch the magic. You weren't put on this earth to break even. You're here to break rules, break records, and breakthrough.

People ask me, "How did you do it? How did you change your life? How did you just leave everything behind to start living the life of your dreams?"

I just woke up one day and decided I didn't want to just survive anymore, I wanted much more, at home, in business, in my relationships. So, I decided I needed change. Just like that.

We have a chance to decide what we become, what we think about all day, and to know you have a choice to change those thoughts at any point in time. Every day is a new day to get started.

I hear many superstars to this day say they are nervous as all shit when they go out on stage, and they go through the same as what we all go through if you listen to their stories. No one person is better than you it is just we put people on Pedder stools as authorities in their fields. The tip is you have the freedom to pull the superstar card anytime, as we were all born superstars. We naturally want to retreat but we know that will not serve us.

Remember: it's the small changes, adding new habits, build on this term habit stacking, one day at a time to live your extraordinary life however that looks for you as it is about you - Superstar.

Once you have mastered a new habit, stack another one and another until you are feeling more fulfilled and now thriving.

Change takes courage, and courage is not something you attend a workshop and you acquire overnight. Courage is an internal force and it's just listening to your body and feelings, and being directed to what that thing is, your vision as you get closer.

Use your support network and if you feel you don't have one find that trusted advisor you can talk to.

Self-appreciation is important as without that no one can grow, without knowing who they truly are. Then just take a minute to think about all the people who loved us in to being who we are today. No one needs the approval of others to be their authentic selves. It is your journey to be all that you are truthfully.

I found journaling got me to a place where I could really do much self-expression. You don't need to be a writer to get your message on paper. This message may just be for you or you may want to share with the world as I am today.

Get the work done on self so that you can express yourself in truth, coming from the heart. I would find myself getting caught up in others business and still do but now catch myself doing it.

If you regret a lost (or found) relationship, a career choice, a financial decision, an educational experience, then instead of focusing on "what if I had," focus on "what I want." You can't revisit the past, but you can turn your attention to something you want.

So, this career isn't the best one; how do you paint a picture of something you do want?

So, the person you let get away got away; how do you create a life you can enjoy as a single person? Paint a picture in as much detail as you can about where you'd like to head.

This will start turning your attention away from the rear-view mirror and to the windshield looking forward.

Become entranced today. Turn your attention to your senses. smell, taste, hear, and enjoy whatever it is you are doing at a greater level than you have done before. Really engage with your world.

Notice things you haven't noticed before and resolve to be PRESENT with whatever is going on. As Oprah Winfrey said, "Whatever has happened to you in your past has no power over this present moment because life is now."

Get involved with the now and heighten your senses to what is around you.

The mind cannot focus on two things at once, so if you turn your attention to your surroundings, you won't be able to focus on your rear-view regrets. Regret can, in fact, spur us to action. We just need to be ready and notice that is what the feeling is about.

If you keep driving with your eyes on what you have left behind, you are bound to eventually crash. Take the steps to get your eyes back on the road and see the scenery of today and focus on where you are going.

Whenever something doesn't work out the way you thought it would, instead of thinking that something went wrong, see it as something that went unexpectedly well, but for reasons that are not yet apparent.

I now work on trust and being true to myself. My truth changes my life immediately.

Which brings me to narratology and comparative mythology, the monomyth, or the hero's journey, is the common template of a broad category of tales and lore that involves a hero who goes on an adventure, and in a decisive crisis wins a victory, and then comes home changed, or transformed.

The 'Hero's journey'

The "Hero's Journey" is the common thread amongst all amazing characters (and stories) in life. Your soul is calling you. It is telling you that you have a unique path that only you can take. Your mind can rationalise all sorts of reasons why you shouldn't take the not yet journeyed path.

Hero's journey is filled with lessons, hardships, heartaches, joys, celebrations and special moments that will ultimately lead us to our destination, our purpose in life. The road will not always be smooth; in fact, throughout our travels, we will encounter many challenges.

Some of these challenges will test our courage, strengths, weaknesses, and faith. Along the way, we may stumble upon obstacles that will come between the paths that we are destined to take.

In order to follow the right path, we must overcome these obstacles. Sometimes these obstacles are really blessings in disguise, only we don't realise that at the time. How we react to what we are faced with determines what kind of outcome the rest of our journey through life will be like.

When things don't always go our way, we have two choices in dealing with the situations. We can focus on the fact that things didn't go how we had hoped they would and let life pass us by, or two, we can make the best out of the situation and know that these are only temporary setbacks and find the lessons that are to be learned.

Time stops for no one, and if we allow ourselves to focus on the negative, we might miss out on some really amazing things that life has to offer.

Sometimes you are going to need to walk away from what you know. You are going to have to face your fears, improve your conditioning, and create your own unique path. You are going to feel scared, excited, and alive!

It never ends whilst we are having our human experience. All those things and people that shape you, showed you the person you are today.

Remember everything that makes you who you are today is actually perfect. Just switch the story if you need to. Your story is one that can and will inspire someone else in this world.

You have a purpose to why you exist, why you live, why you breathe, why you were placed in the town or city that you grew up in, to be raised the way that you are.

I now know the feeling between living an ordinary life and an extraordinary life, the one you can thrive in. The one you wake-up every day and think, what can I do today to make the world a better place. Who can I serve today?...

Daily habits to reclaim your life

Declutter, buy flowers, light a candle, play music, light some sage...

Nurture yourself in whatever feels good to you. Either extra sleep, exercise, meditation, comfort food, laughter, hugs, purchase for self a little gift...Just love yourself UP!

Show your INNER CHILD some love and attention. Even if you find a photo of yourself between ages three to nine and spend time connecting with the innocent version of you.

What does your inner child need to hear? What does he/she need to heal? Look at the photo and repeat, "I see you; I love you; all is okay." Then say, "Do you know how I know this? Because I am here living it."

Play with your imagination in positive ways. Visualise your desired outcomes and get a sense of what it feels like to achieve your dreams.

Join a club or do something you enjoy. Gardening is where I started and actually wasn't what I thought I enjoyed, far from it, but what it taught me to do was slow down to smell the roses which is what I was seeking. Yes, I grow roses now!!

Close your eyes and create a mind movie of how your dreams are playing out right now.

Whilst we generally use this for worrying, so much more powerful to use for manifesting your BEST LIFE.

Place your hand on your heart and repeat the following." I deeply and completely LOVE, honour, accept and forgive myself. I am worthy of deep love."

Surrender and know that even though change is hard, it is always an invitation to up-level our skills in life.

To work with anxiety and other emotions - Do grounding exercise, walk in nature, limit the amount of news/social media/take a magnesium supplement, focus on deep breaths.

Drink more water and take long baths, rest, journal, do yoga, wear loose clothing and slow down. Go with the flow.

One's life has value so long as one attributes value to the life of others, through love, friendship, indignation and compassion. Remember we are not walking this path alone. Your story is one that can and will inspire others in the world. Are you ready to tell it?

To have JOY in our lives
is a universal desire
just like our desire
for water, food,
and fresh air

Chapter 8
Finding Your Joy

There are no tears without joy, and there is no joy without tears.

Shlomo Carlebach

Will I know joy when I see it?

We all want joy in our lives. It is a universal desire just as is our want for water, food, and fresh air.

I discuss a little more about my life and how being vulnerable is hard and the challenges I faced opening up about my personal life. I discuss how Life, Love, and Growth play a factor in my journey. The process is powerful, the content is meaningful.

One memory that gifted me the strength to do what I thought was impossible was a result of exposing my vulnerability, feeling vulnerable became my new normal.

I recall it like it was yesterday however it was over a decade ago. We attended an appointment after waiting for six months to see a Genetsis regarding our son who was not meeting his milestones, and deep down we knew something was wrong.

A visit that we had resisted, to find the truth of what lied ahead for us all. I was overwhelmed with the emotion of what was about to unfold.

Then replaying over and over in the coming months and years similar to hearing my father's first words at birth.

I knew within my heart that this was not just a delay in his development it was much more.

We had been doing our own research and working with therapists during this time, but when you get confirmation and hear the actual words, it feels like your heart has been ripped out and punched, then put back for the work it was doing pounding at a rhythm I could not control.

I was having an out of body experience looking blank when the specialist turned to me to say, "Are you okay Karen?" I turned to him and said with my first face/mask on, yes, of course, holding back the tears thinking what his life will be like, and what does this mean for us all. My first question does this mean his life could be shortened? What do we need to know about his health implications?

I recall what followed to be told your child has this condition, and no one knows what the future holds, just go home and love him, as he is Dylan before Williams Syndrome which was his primary diagnosis. The final comment before we left his office his parting note was, "I will leave you with this thought, if you were going to have a child with a disability or diagnosis of any syndrome, then this is the best you could ask for as they carry the happy gene."

I do think he was encouraging us to feel some sense of relief, but right now I put on my fake smile and left his office with this new information that we had no idea what to do with. It was like being new parents all over again.

Life's struggles

My façade continued to play out with a little more magnification now for the next five years convincing myself life was good, it could be worse, right? I didn't even allow myself the grieving process, allow my true feelings to surface, the opportunity to process and we were taught, *programmed* when life deals you something, you just get on with it.

So, the next option was what help would our son need and decide the best way forward to do just that, help him and put my thoughts and feelings aside and deal with them later.

Of course, in the perfect world that would have been ideal if I was in the right headspace to do this. I was still damaged remember not even close to being on my way to joy.

Dylan struggled with everyday living on this planet with sensory overload and probably didn't help a mother bumping into walls and the disconnection I still experienced which grew bigger as our lives became more isolated.

The events that took place in my life I knew were what I needed to get me to feel and to take positive action. It does take time, courage and an understanding that life is not what we had planned, but do we even stop to visualise the life we feel we have missed out on?

This was now my opportunity to dig deeper to strengthen my character that had been ignored for 50+ years. Maybe Dylan coming into my life was my gift before a freight train hit me, to do a review of my life, and create some JOY, the joy like myself and everyone deserves.

Tears of joy

I found tears of Joy with my son who I speak about. As I write the way I feel I want to share through my words in the hope that the energy of this story will help others.

I was born into a poor family that was disconnected emotionally. I was told from the minute I was born and the years that would follow that I was ugly, a family that was just surviving, and then the ultimate shame and pain, I felt abandoned by my mother.

Just when I thought happiness was around the corner with a new home, a new state, new start, I soon found out my now ex-husband was a compulsive gambler, lost a large amount of money. I came crashing down again.

You can play the blame game but all that does is create DIS-ease in your body and robs you of your joy.

I have heard people that are grieving for the lost child who died too young or was murdered. Many went on to write books, create workshops and retreats to help other families that have had similar experiences. Many stay victims of their circumstances.

Victimhood

Being the victim is too much pain to bare, being the healer who can share their story and create something to help others going through the same pain, to keep them alive and give meaning to their lives.

In regards to the family I grew up in I realised that I had stayed disconnected because of my experience, and I could stay in the blame game, blame my family how things turned out, be unhealthy, or I can own it and be on the path to forgiveness and live a joyful life as ultimately it is only me that is being deeply affected. In the end I chose JOY!

I stopped fighting the sadness, I stopped judging it, letting it paralyse me. Instead, I would let it wash over me, accepting it, working with it rather than resisting and apologising for it. One memory at a time that surfaced I learnt was to sit with and allow myself to feel into the thought or feeling deeply.

As you know, I found journaling my favourite past time allowing me to heal. I created a space to write whilst tears were flooding my vision. In the past, I would have waited until I felt happy or joyful before I could write anything that I thought others would enjoy, keep it light and positive.

I realised that tears of joy and happiness are one of the same. I soon learnt that as well-being vulnerable showing my vulnerability meant I could turn a 'weakness' into 'strength'.

When we're having a rough time, we often feel like we need to pretend that everything is okay, that everyone will look down on us if we admit what's really going on, shows a sign of weakness, and yet when we do open up, people often respond with empathy & encouragement.

See, the secret everyone is just waiting to hear that they are hurting the same way. Tell your story as a writer, you are the perfect person to do it.

> *"For God's sake, tell us something that will save us from ourselves. Take a deep breath and tell us your deepest, darkest secret, so we can wipe our brow and know that we're not alone."*
>
> **Alan Watts**

Pathway to joy

I did decide that I was ready to embrace the joyful life with much more meaning and depth. Once I made this decision everything which took me, started seeing many fabulous experiences and to see the beauty and joy within.

I have never felt so comfortable with myself and confident in who I am now, and what I can achieve for the greater community. It is a ripple effect. I drew the line in the sand stepped over and closed a few doors. I owed it to myself to come out of this victimhood so I can make a positive difference in the world.

Now I am reconnecting and forgiving myself and others from my past so they and myself can move forward in life. My way of dealing with things that felt uncomfortable was to run and hide (not physically) but emotionally, and still have those days where if I allow things to get on top of me they could turn to shit, or I could step up, confront it and change the dynamics of the situation.

Once we look at these experiences and provide forgiveness for ourselves, and the other person, a big weight is lifted. I now know this was my lot to strengthen my foundations to go forward in life with a much bigger picture, a vision far greater than me. Like filling a big pair of shoes, you will grow into them. I was learning to just be myself, enJOY every facet of life, and stay connected.

It is truly exhilarating and requires time spent working on all areas in our lives that is holding us back, those things that no longer serve us as we grow. We can't respond the same way as a nine-year-old, when we are fifty-seven as in my case. It just doesn't work.

Change is imminent. I was living a restricted life allowing everything that happened to me seem like someone was out to get me.

The experiences with my upbringing led me to the failure to my first marriage, alcohol fuelled arguments in relationships and trust was something I had lost.

Once I took control of my finances, I soon worked out that my lesson was to be in control and own my stuff. I couldn't save my ex-husband, however I could free him to meet someone that would be financially more independent rather than me who was dependent upon someone else to manage the money.

The expression I have used in my book that life does not happen to you it happens for you is applicable in every aspect.

A son who needed care beyond the years of a typically developing child. I realised to do this required me to be present, build on the strength in my character, grow patience, and a sense of humour.

The number one thing he showed me that I spent my life searching out there for love, he showed me the way back to my heart.

We are being presented opportunities, some subtle and others in your face. The trick is to recognise these opportunities or circumstances as a gift, generally we say why me or everything seems to always happen to me. What about the expression when given a lemon, make lemonade. There is always another way or another perspective. Be kind to yourself.

You only you can be the change and you have got this. Step up and own it and be your true self no matter the cost.

Addressing all areas, we are challenged with requires a tremendous amount of courage. For the moment most of us are either making the choice to protect ourselves from conflict, discomfort, and vulnerability by staying quiet. Either way, the choices we are making to protect our beliefs can leave us disconnected, afraid and lonely.

The disconnection I felt was keeping me away from what I needed to achieve.

I knew I didn't want to stay in fear and feel discomfort. I certainly was not quiet, but I knew my message needed to be clearer and more concise to make a positive difference. I didn't want to hide from the world anymore.

"I define connection as the energy that exists between people when they feel seen, heard, and valued; when they can give and receive without judgment; and when they derive sustenance and strength from the relationship." "Courage starts with showing up and letting ourselves be seen."

Brene Brown

Do I have a purpose, or do I keep leaving a blazing trail of sadness behind me? That's why a deep connection to your purpose and an undying persistence to achieve what is inside your heart is paramount to your success on the planet. This is a gift. Unwrap the gift that will ultimately bring the meaning of joy into your life.

Making sure what is within you emerges out into the light and shine so bright. To make sure you grow the business, the movement, the foundation that you care about, to make sure that you make the most of every single minute of your life, and to make sure that you use the gifts within you to help humanity in the best way you know how.

As soon as you offer your time to help or want to make a difference in the world you will find strength and resilience in the deepest moments of weakness.

Your purpose will refuel you when you are on the verge of giving up and draw signs and solutions to you right when you need them.

Without it, you will feel weak in the face of the greatest opportunities of your life instead of the courageous, resilient, and powerful human being that you were born to be.

The absence of your purpose will leave you feeling lost and defeated by life.

So, be the champion of your own life.

Be the champion who pursues their purpose and fights their battles with gumption. The champion who looks for the light in the darkness, The champion who lives and works from their heart and soul, The champion who continues to renew their faith that life has a plan for them and is working on their side.

That determination to give yourself an extraordinary life and help others do the same is what will carry you through the greatest storms and the roughest seas… to the fulfilment of your destiny.

I agree, we all need a little "double rainbow" magic in our lives … maybe we won't be screaming about how happy we are like the rainbow, but something that provides us with that awe feeling is a great space.

I had no idea until the last few years that I could control my own life that I alone could make the decision whether good or bad and knew the outcomes would lie solely with me! That I owned it, all of it.

Daily habits to reclaim your life

You can look back at the successes and failure of the past year. You can visualise and set new hairy bodacious goals and what I learnt is that you can start your new beginning anytime, just get started.

We all want to be happy and joyful. It is a desire as our want for water, food, and fresh air.

But happiness is a difficult thing to measure. It is a spectrum, not an absolute. There is a whole science behind our happiness levels, why they fluctuate, and what we can do to boost them.

Ironically, too much time and thought spent in the pursuit of happiness has been found to decrease a person's overall happiness. It is an inside job.

Pivotal moments - Look at the turning points in your life and list those (i.e. bullied at school, lack self-worth, the marriage failed, feeling abandoned and alone)

Writing/journaling - Believe it or not, you can write your way to happiness. Physically writing down your feelings on paper, helps your brain process and eliminate the negatives ones, leaving you more joyful.

Smile, or better yet, strike up a conversation with a stranger. I talk to someone I do not know every day. Make it a new habit. Be conscious and do it on purpose then it will become quite the norm.

Stop Saying "I'm Sorry" Science tells us that those of us who avoid apologies are happier than those who own up to their blunders. Refusing to apologise gives us a sense of power and entitlement.

Volunteer - In helping others, you also help yourself. That's because altruism is proven to boost happiness. So, spend some time volunteering for a community or charity. The more often you give back, the more self-satisfaction you will receive

Exercise - A shot of endorphins to the brain will make you feel oh-so-good. And one of the best ways of getting this boost is with exercise. Do what floats your boat, running, soccer, ice skating, a long walk in the park or by the water if that is possible. Get moving and get instant satisfaction.

Practice Forgiveness – By offering someone our forgiveness — no matter how terrible the offence seems and how much you feel resistance — we let go of the hurt and anger that person stirred in us, thereby creating more space for happier emotions.

Remember it is never about you. On our journey to collect joy from our everyday surroundings, we must also dispose of any residual negativity. Saying, "I forgive you," is a great start. If you cannot say it to the person say it out loud it has the same impact.

This is not an exhaustive list, drinking water, self-love, eat more fruit and vegetables, or supplementation has to be at the top of the list to get your overall well-being functioning at its optimum. We need to look after all of us.

Make a list of times in the past year you laughed so hard you were in physical pain.

Make another list of events in the past year that made you so excited you could not sleep.

Do it and do it for the rest of your life.

In order to stand in your power, you *must* allow yourself the option of saying NO

Chapter 9

Stand In Your Own Power

"To be yourself in a world that is constantly trying to make you something else is the greatest accomplishment."

Ralph Waldo Emerson

Our greatest gift is our power

I had given up my power because I didn't know who I was. I wore a mask for the world to see as I had lost my own identity being a victim of my own circumstances.

Knowing who you are is so much more than just knowing what you do and not do. It is knowing the things in life that activate you, and the things that don't.

Being in tune with your emotions, knowing when you need to step away and take a breather. All of these things and so much more all play a part in knowing yourself.

The word 'power can be perceived as control over other people, or money, or even forcefully influencing the course of events. That is the dictator way to define power, but there is another definition and the one we are talking about is the ability to act effectively.

For example, there is the power of speech or the basic power of saying no to what you do not want and yes to what you do want.

To stand in your own power means to honour what is important to you. It means you know who you are, what you are capable of, and why you make the decisions you make. Nothing can shake the foundation of who you truly are.

Become aware of the root of your sense of powerlessness. Before you construct the next narrative on who is stealing your power, get curious about the underlying feelings of powerlessness that precede all situations.

But let's face it, most of us get in our way. I made it about me in that I was unattractive and unworthy. I was destroying something that was already perfect.

We indulge in self-doubt, self-sabotage, and mind games like "I don't deserve this," or "I'm not good enough." Are you scared of what others will think or say about you?

Do you feel overwhelmed by your situation, or inadequate to handle the complexities of your daily task list? Do you keep sabotaging your own success?

A good indicator that you are not standing in your own power making you powerless, giving your power away.

It is easy to give away your power. Do you let your partner make all the decisions such as where you eat, or which movie, or show you see? Do you say no to your kids' demands? Do you take on whatever you are asked to do, no matter how full your plate is already? Do you validate your own thoughts and feelings to please others? What or who are you allowing to rule your life?

Pleasing others is a habit. You probably developed it when you were very young when you learned that being cute or using good manners or getting good grades made your parents happy and that made you feel good.

When power is taken away

Maybe you had to push away your own needs to fit into your family. You learned to keep your opinions, thoughts, and emotions to yourself. You the real you were silenced.

You followed the crowd rather than making waves. You learned to give away your power for the approval of others. *At what cost? You denied your own voice, the authentic you.*

So, how do you stop giving your power away? Before you agree to volunteer your services when you have a looming work deadline, STOP, and ask yourself what you really want, then honour that.

In order to stand in your power, you *must* allow yourself the option of saying no. It doesn't matter what others think about you. It doesn't matter if your family or friends get upset with you. You simply cannot do it all without hurting yourself.

At some point, all of us face the choice of either claiming our power or giving it away.

Focus on what is right for *you*. Quit worrying about what other people think of you. Have the courage to stand up for yourself. Dare to endure criticism from others.

Be willing to shock the people who assume you will always comply with whatever they ask of you.

Standing in your power doesn't mean that you must be perfect. It means that you accept yourself as you are, your weaknesses and your strengths, your smart actions and your foolish blunders no matter what anyone else thinks.

Do not think you have to wait until you feel ready or worthy. Remember, no matter what you do, some people simply will not like you, you will never be able to make everyone happy.

> *It's not your job to like me, it is mine*
>
> **Bryon Katie**

When you don't take care of yourself because you are trying to make others happy, you start to resent the very people you are trying to please.

Whenever the situation arises where you must decide about what to do, ask yourself this question: Am I standing in my power, or am I trying to please someone else? Be clear about your priorities.

Don't play the martyr

What is more important than your own balance, harmony, and health? Simply put: Don't be a martyr! We all know those unfortunate souls who bend over backwards to make others happy when everyone can see that they are ignoring their own needs.

It is the mother bothered by problems and anxiety, whose kids look impeccable while she hasn't washed her hair in a week, and her clothes look like they came out of the dirty laundry basket.

Martyrs do not love or nurture themselves. You, on the other hand, do!

Pleasing someone else is not the same as caring for them. It is an old story. If you're not caring for yourself, you will have nothing left, no inner resources, to really care for another.

You must learn to stand in your own power for your own mental, physical, emotional, and even your spiritual health!

I spent my whole life hiding because I believed I was unattractive, unworthy, disconnected, and trying to find someone, or something out there tangible to cling to.

Drawn like a moth to a flame to any articles, resources, teachers, and books that will shed some much-needed light on that thing you feel is missing. You spend every waking moment searching for the missing link. Looking around every corner, every unturned stone for happiness.

Whether you are attending personal development workshops or reading the latest self-help books, you can't get enough of this material searching high and low for any inkling of what that missing link might be for you and your life. You might even be spending time at work perusing the web in search of your answer.

I will tell you a secret, the answer you are seeking is not on any website, it lies within you.

Let us go deeper

You feel disconnected from life. Your life is good for the most part, but you cannot help but feel disconnected from the passion and excitement that others feel about their work and life in general. The deepest part of you knows it is possible, but you just aren't sure where to begin.

You are unhappy. From the outside looking in you are living the dream with a good job, enough money, and maybe even a family, but you just cannot shake the unhappiness that lies just under the surface. You cannot quite put your finger on it, but something feels "off" as you wonder, **"Is this it?"**

You may even feel guilty for having those thoughts because there are so many other people in the world that don't have what you do. But despite all that, you know you were meant for more.

You are playing it safe. At one point you had big dreams and aspirations that made you feel excited and alive, but that was before you decided it was easier to just play it safe and live life by the rules. Rules that told you to study, get a good job, save for retirement, take care of your family, and live happily ever after. Only you're not.

You want something more but afraid of the uncertainty that lies on the other side of your dreams and every time you begin to think it's possible, you snap back to reality and recommit yourself to doing what is safe.

Be comfortable with the discomfort. While you know you were meant for bigger and better things, you have become comfortable with the discomfort because you at least know what to expect.

You know that your desires will ebb and flow and that just as you build the courage to do something about your unhappiness, fear creeps in and causes you to retreat back into your normal, logical, live-by-the-rules-life, and we just rinse and repeat the cycle. Crazy right?

You are not doing what you love. This is the biggest sign of them all. If you are not doing what you love, you are not living the life your soul intended. Period.

If you resonate with the signs above, it is time you did something about it, starting today. You have a gift to give to the world and when you are not living the life your soul intended, you are withholding the very gift that will change the world for the better.

People say it is amazing that you are writing a book I could never do that. Can I tell you I thought the same, and here I am? My calling was to get this message out to as many people I know.

Whilst writing this chapter there is a near pandemic global Corona Virus across 90 countries upending routines, threatening livelihoods and prompting quarantines in its spread. This is creating fear something that if we are standing in our own power is impossible to be affected.

We do not want to buy into these fears, the very fears that keep us in an unhealthy state of mind allowing someone or something out there to control us. The very fears that drive us to be medicated.

Daily habits to reclaim your life

Set boundaries for yourself. It is fantastic to hear you are such a giving and loving person. Many times, I hear, but I have so much love to give, I do so much for everyone, and I do not get any of it back.

The secret is to set boundaries in what you give away. Everything that you grant to other people, you should never expect back. If you give, it means that you are not expecting anything in return.

Expecting something in return means to exchange and could be viewed as labour for love.

Let your passion lead you to your purpose. Be honest with yourself about what your passions are. What really lights you up and makes you happy?

What would you do if money were not a concern and you weren't afraid? Let your passion lead you to your purpose.

Find a way to do it. Once you decide what makes you happy, find a way to do that now. Not tomorrow, not next week, and certainly not when you retire.

Life is to be lived and enjoyed each and every facet and every moment. Whether you start writing for fun, volunteer, or start a new business, take some action today. Your passion will catapult you forward to more of the same and in no time, you will find yourself living the life of your dreams!

Get help. Chances are if you haven't been living the life your soul intended, you have some major fears and blocks that are holding you back. Seek the help of a professional coach or mentor to help you move through those challenges so you can clearly define what you want (and are meant to do) and gain the support you will need to make it happen.

I enlisted many over the years and even my Book Coach Emily Gowor to keep me accountable and provide support and resources for this read.

Life is too short not to do what you love, and when you are living the life your soul intended, you will experience freedom and bliss you never thought possible.

"Meditation gives us peace of mind without a tranquillizer. And unlike a tranquillizer, the peace of mind that we get from meditation does not fade away. It lasts for good in some corner of the inmost recesses of our aspiring heart."

Sri Chinmoy

The life I was living playing by the rules and putting on a face for the world to see was not for me. The journey to self-discovery started small by not listening to the news, or some random TV show which is looking into the lives of others, so we avoid our own.

Spend time with something that will create a smile with satisfaction. I recall waking up one day, and saying out loud, 'enough now'. This meant creating new daily habits and then seeing this through as a lifelong journey.

Nothing else was working so I didn't want to keep showing up the same every day, worrying about what others think of me and living a life that was a lie really if I was brutally honest.

It is exhilarating to now be myself, after years of hiding I actually now enjoy standing out where for many years would hide, now I speak up, where I deem it necessary. Where I am in service to others to help them improve their existence, to inspire, to give you permission to be who you are.

The natural process of this along the way will be a little disruptive I can guarantee this.

In the past I was coming from anger and fear, so the results were not pretty as I felt the need to prove myself, justify why I did, or said something creating a situation where outcomes would be somewhat destructive.

You are ready for this change and know you will never look back. I find I am now thriving rather than just surviving. My path of disruption has allowed me the opportunity to see myself in a different light, which is now shining like a beacon.

Collectively we *can* make a difference to others lives with much work to be done to unfear those that live with fear.

Disruption to life is very healthy because we need to challenge the status quo. We need to question our thoughts and we need to be the change and be mindful, be consistent in your daily rituals in your pursuit to a full life in service to others.

I am prepared to lose people in my life, or more appropriately set them free as happiness is important for everyone. Some people do not want to be set free for fear of the unknown.

I now face my fears head-on, however, still have avoidance days that show that we're human but be prepared to do what it takes now. Mission not impossible.

How far you go in life rests largely on how deep your courage to be yourself is, no matter what the world around you might say.

Shine your unique light! The world needs the authentic you, not the version constrained by other opinions of you. Do not reduce yourself to fit in.

It can be scary to show up authentically; we humans are social animals and we instinctively worry about being rejected. Just remember:

No matter how big or small you play, other people will have an opinion anyway, so you may as well be yourself.

Other people's opinions of you are really none of your business. Always stay in your own business/power.

There are plenty of other tribes out there; the authentic you will attract your people. Find your tribe they are out there.

How is the authentic you going to surface this week?

People are often so afraid of what people's opinions of them might be that they hold back from their dream or give up on it altogether. They waste precious time that could otherwise be spent on what truly matters, their purpose, and, in doing so, they miss out on the extraordinary life that is possible for them.

But here is the thing no one makes an impact on the world without doing things differently.

Great individuals don't fit in. They are unlike anyone else. To be great, to fly, to rise to the top in life, you must be willing to stand out - to be the one-of-a-kind design that you were born to be.

It is in breaking the mould, not in trying to cut off or change parts of ourselves to fit in, that we discover that there is no one else like us and that this is a magnificent thing.

If we follow the crowd and give up who we are in order to belong, we may never discover our path and place in the world. We will live our entire life in hiding instead of cherishing our originality and all that makes us different.

But when you take heed of the cues from within you that guide you to the fulfilment of your purpose, you will experience a depth of meaning during your time on Earth that will make you wonder why you waited so long to be faithful to what your soul yearns to do.

Unrivalled personal power rests in your courage to be original and reclaim your unique role in the world. You are not just rare: you are one in several billion.

No one can be you, beat you, compete with you, or replace you once you truly own that. It is what enables you to find your competitive advantage, your original difference, and play your winning hand in life by doing what you do best and love the most.

Always remember you are a work of art and it is time to realise that you truly are perfection made manifest so that the world can benefit from the highest expression of your soul and your entire life can flourish in the process.

Don't deny yourself or anyone else of who you are and what you offer. Go get em, tiger.

I could not turn to religion,
my family or a therapist -
so I was forced to turn
to myself

Chapter 10
Create The Life You Desire

"Let them go. Your destiny is never tied to anyone who leaves you. And it doesn't mean they're bad people. It just means that their part of the story is over."

Julia Roberts

It's your future that counts

You may have some serious wreckage from your past, but you have a choice today about how you think about your future.

Pessimism may run through your family tree as it did mine, but you can break the lineage with changing the way you think.

I was desperately seeking something outside of myself. I was never told there was another way even though I knew with every fibre of my being there was more, more depth to my character, more that I can share with others, and to build the confidence around making a difference and showing up.

I was stuck in my mind, and in darkness as my life experiences led me to crisis point, a friendship that I no longer wanted to be a part of.

I had allowed myself to get embroiled in a friendship that was controlling me again, someone that judged me. We never left on bad terms but as I changed, she phased out of my life which I now know was the best thing for both of us.

I felt alone again, I couldn't turn to religion, my family or therapist so I was forced to turn to myself. I was never told there was another way, but I'm here to tell you with what I know now, there is. You know that to be true now too.

Being in the driver seat

I cannot describe the feeling that washed over me once I came to terms with who I am and being okay to not fit in, and just be yourself without justification, to be in control of your destiny.

These thoughts which seemed quite scary or overwhelming however when I look back at my previous life as I refer to it, to think that might be how I would continue to live would be denying myself to share with you what I now know to be true.

Life, to be the driver of your own vehicle, your mind, body and soul, and not even considering what others think about you as this is your life, your business, and nobody else has a say in the matter.

Being in control rather than operating by default and looking back thinking what I did with my life has got to be more appealing. The people you get to spend your days with who are inspiring, attractive, more appealing. These people I would have always aspired to be, who some I now work alongside. There is not one person who is better, or greater than us.

When we get out of our own way, we can achieve more in the greater community, and for the good of mankind, and begin to live the life that we signed up for.

Living an ordinary life to me meant I was just the same as everyone else, I knew that not to be true, I knew I was different, but in what way. I was missing the building blocks to show me there *was* another way.

> "If you are always trying to be normal you will never know how amazing you can be"
>
> **Maya Angelou**

> "The truth is most people aren't living an extraordinary life. They're drifting through life without really knowing where they're going or what they want. As a result, their relationships, income, health, activities, and behaviours are pretty mediocre."
>
> **Anthony Moore**

We do need to be willing to live this extraordinary life, do it on our terms and by your own rules.

You cannot live the life you want to live if you go on to believing that success is what everyone else says it is. I am telling you as I learnt the hard way! And you cannot expect to live the life you want by showing up today the same you, that you were yesterday.

I did not define success on my own terms. I chose to do what others expected of me rather than finding out for myself what I really wanted.

I, like many of my generation, left schools early, I had no idea what I wanted to do for the rest of my life and took up the first job which was my Thursday evening and Saturday morning job offered as fulltime regardless of how I felt about it. It seemed the right thing to do. "Just get a job and pay your way through life, they said."

Now sometimes you do need to do this based on decisions you are making at that moment with the tools/skills you have, however it should not be forever.

Make it a steppingstone to either build that business, or that amazing job opportunity that fits your passion, that things that ignite you. Do not waste time on achieving something that you don't want to do, and in the process building someone else's dream.

> *"Your level of success will seldom exceed your level of personal development, because success is something you attract by the person you become."*
>
> **Jim Rohn**

We need to consider during this process to success, the building blocks, which are our VITALS

Happiness. You will be happier when you can express who you are. Expressing your desires will make it more likely that you get what you want.

Less inner conflict. When your outside actions are following your inside feelings and values, you will experience less inner conflict.

Better decision-making. Knowing yourself means you can make better choices, from small decisions such as what will I wear today, to the much bigger decisions like who will I spend my life with. You will have guidelines you can apply to solve life's varied problems

When you know yourself, you understand what motivates you to resist bad habits and develop good ones. You will have the insight to know which values and goals activate your willpower.

Resistance to social pressure. When you are grounded in your values and preferences, you are less likely to say "yes" when you want to say "no."

Vitality and pleasure. Being who you truly are helps you feel more alive and makes your experience to live richer, more expansive, and more exciting. To get that you have got to constantly improve, and watch as your mindset begins to expand, and the world begins to bend, and you start to thrive.

The exciting bit is because you're making it happen for yourself. The more you do the more you want. You will become an expert at personal development, more reading, listening to audios, watching what you eat so being healthier and wanting to exercise.

"Always dream and shoot higher than you know you can do. Do not bother just to be better than your contemporaries or predecessors. Try to be better than yourself."

William Faulkner

Be that person who evolves every day into a new version of themselves, stay unstuck and become that person you want to be.

Keep on swimming upstream so a little force or feeling of resistance is good as you know it's helping. Not too much your exhausted and like going to the gym you go hard to quick and you don't go back.

It takes time then sit with any decision before going to the next level. Creating those new habits and stack em up, tiger. You have got this, and I believe in you.

Just be constant and vigilant knowing and recognising the feeling when those changes happen, when your days flow freely, and people, things are attracted to you. It just is, and I can't explain and why would I as that is my experience, you will get to have your own.

What advice I did take, was to act as if you're living the life you want to be living, and soon you will be doing just that. It is a system and if you are consistent you will start achieving the life you want to live.

You have the rest of your life and every day is another chance to change it.

"No matter what happens or bad it seems today life does go on, and it will be a better tomorrow."

Maya Angelou

Convinced?

Daily habits to reclaim your life

Let's do this

Every time a thought pops into your head that does not serve you, replace it with one that does. For example, instead of thinking *I hate my body*. Think, *I deserve to feel good, so I am going to make healthy choices today*. Or instead of thinking, *nobody likes me.* Think, *the people that matter like me.*

It really does work however it is a skill that requires daily input. To catch yourself when you have a thought that makes you question it, as you are now on the path to living this extraordinary life, a life you desire, because you are amazing right? Yes!

Let's keep journaling our new language towards being kind rather than unkind to ourselves as being kind to ourselves and others is the greatest gift one can give to themselves and others.

What we think about we believe to be true, as that is all we have known up to now right?

Depending upon how old you are, and how long your stories have been running inside you. The secret which is not really a secret, however, start questioning those thoughts that are leaving you feeling empty.

Why am I feeling angry, resentful etc? Write down the things, or people by name and the word that expresses how you feel towards those things that is far cry from making you smile.

The clearer we get, as they are only thoughts, that if we believe those things to be wholeheartedly true then we are buying into it, something we believe to be true we **will** buy into.

Decisions you make now will evolve in the future, it is same as goal setting but personal goals, and you revisit them regularly to make sure you are on track in achieving your life goals.

There is no right or wrong, or restrictions, we are only restricted by the limitations we place on ourselves. These are decisions based on the tools (knowledge) or vitals you have in your skillset/tool bag right now.

You can upgrade your skills anytime, by studying personal development, reading, listening to audios, attending workshops anything you are drawn to. Even purchasing that favourite outfit. Your needs and wants to be met.

My husband is very generous and supportive, never questions anything I do however a line he has in his repertoire if I ask for his advice on anything really is, love it madly, need it badly, or don't buy, or do it.

For me to come back to myself and know that we will always be okay. You will be okay.

The key to unlocking my mind was to question my thoughts, to connect with my own identity, to trust, to know we are not alone on this journey. What is it for you?

I now know that being connected, being part of a community was my saviour if I stay connected. For most of us, this is the key to unlock the door to freedom. I choose 'connection' over 'disconnection'.

I forgive those in my life and in fact thank them now because without them I may never have discovered in this lifetime, and lived with regrets, rather now live a life by design.

I forgive myself for sabotaging my life and know it was a process I had to go through. There is a greater force out there just waiting to help us.

I also ask you to invite your resentments on a piece of paper, your own personal work, private work, just short simple sentences.

No one else needs to see or know these that is up to you if you wish to share. You can read back to yourself, then if you can forgive them and yourself for that feeling it created for you in the body and know that your response was coming from how you felt with a similar experience as a child.

You are no longer that child you are now an adult, so we now respond as an adult or at the age, we are now with a different set of skills/mindset.

Once we take responsibility and are held accountable for our actions, we can create more control in our lives. From here the recovery process is in motion! Also, create your own dialogue that resonates with you, create definite main purpose statements (DMPS) that work and stay with the Change them where you need to.

I love my daily main purpose statements. I have included a list in this chapter which is not exhaustive and changes over time.

They are just suggestions to help you write your own. Start somewhere and develop as you go.

Run through them consistently twice daily before you jump out of bed, and when you are resting in bed before sleep, which I found was a nice time where there are no demands placed on you.

Other times, when a negative thought enters your mind, don't dismiss it, just say to yourself that was the old way of thinking, I don't think that way anymore, and replace with a DPMS.

If you feel/think about something positive, it is impossible to think something negative. Try it. ☺

"I am so blessed to have amazing people in my life who are always supporting me."

"I am an unstoppable warrior who is strong and fearless."

"I live with courage and compassion in my heart."

"I wear my confidence like a shield to deflect all negativity."

"I am powerful and proud of who I am and what I do."

"I wake up each day positive and ready to take on the day ahead because I am on a mission to achieve my goals and nothing and no one can stop me!"

"I am at the top of my game."

Change does need to come from a place of LOVE.

Sharing words by Emily Gowor

[You can't silence the calling for greatness within you]

Deep down in the very core of you, you KNOW that you are capable of being, doing, and having more in your life.

You know that you are worthy of it,

That you have so much more inside you yet,

That you are just warming up in fulfilling your purpose,

That you are not here to settle for an average existence,

That you are extraordinary in your very essence, And,

That you are only scratching the surface of what's possible for you.

That knowing that you feel is the calling for greatness that exists inside each one of us.

No matter what twists and turns your life's journey takes you on or where you might find yourself, that calling to be exactly who you are lives on, strong inside you.

The separation between where you are and where you would love to be will keep pulling at you, like a child tugging on your coat, vying for your attention, until you decide to do what you love every day.

Any misalignment between what you do daily and what your heart is calling you to do will continue to unsettle you until you decide to make time for what truly matters.

It never goes away – that yearning from your SOUL for a greater life.

That voice inside you never dies down – the one leading you to the fulfilment of your purpose on planet Earth.

Your heart never stops beating for your craft,

It never stops yearning for time spent on what you care about most,

And, it never stops aching for the pursuit of what inspires you.

The fastest path to the deep sense of meaning and a life full of significant moments is to give yourself over to that calling: the calling to devote your entire self to YOUR calling.

It is to give up ideas of what you think you are meant to do and surrender any reasons you think what you want can't or won't happen.

It is to believe more deeply in the possibility for your future than any pain or limitations of your past.

It is to LET GO – of fear, of doubt, of questioning yourself, of disbelief in your own dreams – and let what's INSIDE you guide you.

It is to honour the quiet whispers that speak from your core – and follow them.

It is to allow yourself full immersion in what you feel you were born to do – without hesitation.

To feel your heart – and honour it.

This the doorway through which everything you dream of exists.

And that is the life that you deserve.

When you are unsure of your calling, turn to the one who called you in the first place. I think you know who that person is. Yes, it's YOU, the real you. Welcome home. ☺

Conclusion

Abandonment, controlling, resentment, excuses could be made of course as separated by a power we did not understand. However, wherever we are, we make choices, some foolish ones, or ones that save yourself, or someone else, always in the hope that the goodwill out way the harm.

From the beginning, I never understood that I was living a life as a victim and that there *was* another way, thriving rather than just surviving, allowing others to control me, and living with the feeling of abandonment and resentment from others.

The only way change is ever likely, is to discover and recover who you are, the real you, realise your sense of purpose, and how you can help others create a life they only ever dreamed about, as they fell into the trap of looking up to others, always thinking someone is better or more intelligent, have more than you, those that have what you want, and are changing the world.

I truly believe if we are coming from a space of self-acceptance, accepting where we are right now and that we can change the way we feel and think. Realise those we seek refuge from, are dealing with the same as you. We are no different, we just have a different set of skills which makes us unique and creates an opportunity if we are prepared to see it and understand it.

The best course of action to awaken the potential in others around the world is to offer others the best of what's within you, by doing this you can help awaken them to their best self, to live a life of abundance.

I believe collectively we can bring peace and harmony to the world, to do this we need to identify what we do best, break down the walls that have been built, start by speaking to our neighbours, smile at strangers, meet new people, find your tribe, and contribute to the worlds larger community, to make a difference and leave *your* legacy.

Acknowledgments

Firstly, my appreciation goes to my son Dylan, for igniting my inspiration, for bringing me back to my heart, and providing me with an opportunity to dig deeper than I ever thought possible. To never judge, to lend a helping hand and to be kind to myself.

Also thank you from the depths of my heart to my husband, best friend and life partner in allowing me to recover myself without question. To be by my side, to listen and support always. I love being married to you.

Thank you to my firstborn, my Peter Pan, Matthew for being patient and supporting my dreams even those crazy ones. Thanks for the fun you add in our lives, to always be open to change, and living your own dreams. You have been there longer than anyone I know, and we will always have a special connection.

I would love to express my gratitude to my business partner, friend and mentor Karen Vercoe who was instrumental in pushing me out into the big wide world. Thanks for being encouraging, supportive and for always being there.

Thank you to my dear friend Cheryl Hart who responds to my many crazy requests without question, and offers genius ideas about the design work, and has been part of my writing journey for over ten years now.

To my Photographer Sam Hunter who was very creative with my vision for the picture on the cover of this book.

There are many people I could thank those that have contributed to my life positively. What I say to you is, I love you.

About the Author

Karen Howe is a passionate writer who inspires women facing identity crisis to discover and recover their true identity and own it. Her workshops, books and talks allow women to connect and live a life full of adventures.

After working 20 years in Corporate for only two employers, then being made redundant, feeling disconnected from her family, trust became an issue with the marriage breakup, and left as a single parent believing her life had been carved in stone, soon realised how quickly your power can be taken away at any moment.

Left with uncertainty in life, everything she had believed to be true, and questioning her very own existence, however knowing the one thing she believed to be true was remaining optimistic and having faith.

Karen soon discovered that it was not about the challenges she was faced with it was about having the resilience and the right tools and support in place to live life by design.

Karen loves to inspire others to live with more awesomeness so they can place their focus on opportunities and unlimited possibilities rather than fear and worry.

Her mission in life is not merely to survive, but to thrive; and to do so with passion, compassion, humour and style.

www.karenhowe.com.au

www.ingramcontent.com/pod-product-compliance
Lightning Source LLC
Chambersburg PA
CBHW061404160426
42811CB00114B/2377/J